"*The Foundation of Leadership* provides much-needed insight into the qualities that helped shape America. I highly recommend it."

...**Senator Richard Shelby**,
United States Senator, Alabama

"The moment I played on my first team, I understood the importance of strong, able leadership. No book can teach everything there is to know about leadership, but *The Foundation of Leadership* is an excellent place to begin."

...**Sonny Jurgensen**,
Hall of Fame Quarterback, Washington Redskins

"America has always been a true leader in the world of action and ideas. Such leadership is based on simple, but timeless values that are an essential part of the American spirit. It makes me proud to be an American when I read of the endeavors of the five people who Bo Short writes of in *The Foundation of Leadership*, people who stood up for what was right and utilized their God-given abilities to ensure that America's future is even greater than its past."

...**Armstrong Williams**,
Nationally Syndicated Columnist

"*The Foundation of Leadership* should be required reading for anyone interested in serving this country. Its writing is animated, and the lessons drawn from the discussions of George Washington, John Hancock and others are powerful."

...Lt. General Claudius E. Watts III (Ret),
former President, The Citadel

"No preachment is necessary: The miracle of America began with the faith in their Creator so evident among our Founding Fathers. After reading *The Foundation of Leadership* I am absolutely persuaded that unless and until the American people engage in a revival of that faith — and restore the moral and spiritual principles that evolved from it — the freedoms we so cherish may disappear."

...Senator Jesse Helms,
United States Senator, North Carolina

"*The Foundation of Leadership* is a great source of inspiration and direction for all Americans who aspire to succeed and lead."

...John E. Bianchi,
former Chairman of the Board, Bianchi International

"The hallmark of a true leader is one who never stops learning from others. *The Foundation of Leadership* serves a much-needed purpose by chronicling how some of America's greatest leaders triumphed over adversity. *The Foundation of Leadership* is for students, teachers, coaches, entrepreneurs, parents — or anyone who wants to achieve success in life."

...**Admiral Thomas H. Moorer**,
former Chairman, Joint Chiefs of Staff

"This book captures the essence of why today's citizens need to emulate the leadership qualities of America's Founding Fathers."

...**Dr. Lloyd John Ogilvie**
Chaplain, United States Senate

"*The Foundation of Leadership* manages a difficult feat. It is both a practical, down-to-earth guide for success, and a lofty call to arms for the 'better angels' of our nature."

...**Senator Max Cleland**,
United States Senator, Georgia

EXCALIBUR

PRESS

FOREWORD BY
SENATOR STROM THURMOND

THE FOUNDATION OF LEADERSHIP

Enduring Principles to Govern Our Lives

BO SHORT

EXCALIBUR
PRESS

First published in the United States of America in 1998 by Excalibur
Press, Inc., 107 S. West Street, Suite 137, Alexandria, Virginia 22314

Library of Congress Catalog Card Number: 97-78085

ISBN   0-9658207-0-X

How to Order:
The Foundation of Leadership may be purchased for educational,
business, or promotional use. For information contact Jovita Vergara at
the Russ Reid Company at 202-371-9580, or fax 202-842-3492.

Special Note

100% of the royalties from the sale of this book
are being donated by the author to the
American Leadership Foundation

*Mom, your faith in me has allowed me to believe
that anything I am willing to dream can be accomplished.
Dad, you are an inspiration and a hero to me.
I love you both with all my heart.*

*To my wife, Sandy, and our little girl, Taylor,
I thank God Almighty for bringing both of you into my life.
You are the most precious part of my existence.*

Contents

Foreword

by
Senator Strom Thurmond

As most anyone can imagine the demands placed on a United States Senator are considerable. Between votes, committee hearings, meetings with constituents and briefings, there hardly seems time for one's self or family, let alone honoring outside requests. Due to this schedule it is not common for me to offer to pen the foreword to a literary piece of work. However, this book is quite different as I believe it captures much of the essence of what I consider to be great about America. Additionally, I am pleased to introduce you to the author, Robert "Bo" Short, and the important work he is giving us.

I have had the pleasure of knowing Bo for the past twenty-five years. Over that period I have watched him grow from an inquisitive teenager with a keen mind into a thirty-eight-year-old husband and father who can point to many impressive successes both in his personal and professional life. Not only has he built a lucrative international business but he has done so with an emphasis on his family life. Fate and hard work have truly been kind to my friend.

Though the unseen hand of destiny plays a certain role in how our lives are lived and what we are able to accomplish, the great majority of Bo's successes are directly attributable to the personal qualities and characteristics he possesses. He is unquestionably an individual who has distinguished himself as a leader, a man who is able to communicate and motivate people. I believe that Bo's leadership will have an important impact on this country in the years to come.

For years, during many of our conversations Bo has expressed that one of his passions was the creation of a foundation that would promote leadership in our nation, at every level of society. From the playgrounds of our elementary schools, to the halls of Congress and the boardrooms of corporations, Americans must lead. Whether it is the young boy or girl who sets the example for his or her peers by refusing to succumb to the dangers of drugs and violence, to the public official who takes an unpopular stand as a matter of principle, it is essential for the future and continued prosperity of the United States that our citizens assert uncompromising leadership. It gave me a great sense of pride when I saw that goal of his come to fruition as he created the American Leadership Foundation. This organization is worthy of our support and enthusiasm and I commend Bo for his vision. Additionally, this book serves as an excellent vehicle to introduce you to the principles of the Foundation.

As someone who has served the public for the great majority of my adult life, I have witnessed a multitude of leadership styles. One thing that has always disappointed me is the number of people in leadership positions who are ill-equipped for the responsibilities and demands placed upon them. In many institutions where leadership is absolutely essential to successful operations, there is often a void in this valuable commodity.

During my years in the Senate, I have had the privilege of knowing and working with some great leaders. These individuals understood the importance of service and the impact their decisions had on their fellow citizens. These Senators were found on both sides of the aisle. They were committed to providing an environment of debate and compromise on policy but were never willing to negotiate their principles. I have always found these men and women to posses virtues of true leadership. There is no shame in being an elected official who does not compromise his or her beliefs, but is willing to compromise on a bill in order that the affairs of the nation may move forward. An individual who strikes this balance, at least in Congress, is a person who will usually find themselves in a senior position in the House or Senate someday. It has been my experience that a person who does the same in their private life reaps the rewards of many great successes as well.

For years, people have debated whether true leaders are born or made, but in actuality, it is an argument that is academic as all effective leaders exhibit certain shared characteristics. Whether they are inherited or acquired, refining one's skills as a leader is an ongoing process, as a good leader recognizes that it is always possible to improve. Perhaps one of the most effective ways to become a better leader is to study those who are recognized as being, or having been, successful leaders. From the group of patriots who comprised our Founding Fathers to contemporary captains of industry, we live in a nation that produces individuals who are gifted in leading, as our history is rich with figures who have helped to shape our country.

Without question, there is no greater leader than the Father of our Country, George Washington. He was a military, commercial, and political leader who served the United States during peace and war and made many impressive contributions to society and history. He led our forces to a hard-fought victory over the English, overcoming daunting odds and winning independence for our nation. He helped to shape the Constitution, the finest document ever penned by the mind of man for the governing of a people and which serves as a bedrock of our democracy. As our first president, he helped to unify our new country, as well as setting standards and traditions for the chief executive that are still adhered to today.

As we approach the new millennium, the United States stands as a well-functioning, dynamic, and cohesive nation. However, it was not that long ago that our country was smaller, struggling with its identity, and still largely a land of frontier and uncharted territory. It took men and women of incredible qualities to venture into the unsettled lands and press west toward the Pacific, to build cities in the middle of the plains, to take up arms whenever the nation was threatened, and to create an industrial and economic powerhouse. Americans accomplished these feats because they are a determined people who prize their individualism, covet the opportunity to succeed, and have the guts to take risks. No doubt this is why America produces so many successes in the arts, sports, politics, science, and business, and why the rest of the world looks to us for leadership.

I look to the future with great confidence in the abilities of our young people to continue the wonderful example set by our Founding Fathers. I strongly believe that as they grow older, acquire more skills and life experiences, they will become the individuals who will lead the United States into the 21st century and the best years of our Republic.

Introduction

> *"Important principles may and*
> *must be inflexible."*
> *– Abraham Lincoln*

I grew up in the shadows of the Washington Monument and the Lincoln Memorial in a suburb of our nation's capital. It was there that I began to understand the power of a dream and the belief that it could come true. I saw my father, who was born in a small town in southern Georgia, rise to become the Chief of Staff for the longest serving United States Senator in the history of American politics. My father's perspective on leadership was gained through years of experience interacting with national and international political figures. Having dined with presidents, kings, and heads-of-states, he instilled in me a unique view of America that I will cherish for the rest of my life and pass on to my children.

So much of who we are today is a result of the values instilled in us as children. I vividly remember my parents teaching me the importance of respect for our elders and the difference between right and wrong. I recall words such as loyalty, patriotism, honor, and faith being spoken in my house on countless occasions. I was told that the American flag was to be respected because it was a symbol of the sacrifice that was made for the cause of liberty. My parents instilled in me a conviction that there were things in life worth dying for: our faith, our family, and our country. I remember hearing them speak about America as the only place in the world where anyone could accomplish anything for which they dreamed and worked. I also recall my father saying that, while being an American brought many privileges, these privileges carry, as inseparable companions, heavy responsibilities. Each of us has a duty to ourselves, our children and their children to correct those things that could cause America to stray from her course of freedom and democracy.

"The things that the flag stands for were created by the experiences of a great people. Everything that it stands for was written by their lives. The flag is the embodiment, not of sentiment, but of history." – Woodrow Wilson

It was in this context that I learned about leadership. Leadership was presented as more than a badge one wore while guiding a company or representing a constituency. It was the principles one called upon to govern one's own life. I believe that we must stand together and demand honorable leadership from those we would follow. Most importantly, we must accept nothing less than honorable leadership from ourselves.

In my role as president of the American Leadership Foundation, I have been blessed to spend time in the company of great leaders. I am proud of the fact that many of them serve on the Foundation's Board of Advisors (see Acknowledgments). One of the privileges afforded me in this capacity is the opportunity to interview the men and women that we, as a nation, look to as leaders. Whether in business, politics, the arts, or sports, the leadership and success principles they talk about are the same. Words such as discipline, truth, risk, problem-solving, service, and flexibility are referred to quite frequently. However, regardless of their fields of expertise, they all speak about the role that vision, courage, perseverance, responsibility, and character play in successful leadership.

These five words have served as the pillars on which the American Leadership Foundation has been built. They also serve as the theme of this book. In its preparation, I asked several esteemed members of the United States Senate to share their views on two topics: leadership and America's rise to greatness. Because many of their responses speak eloquently to the theme of this book, I have taken the liberty of quoting them directly.

On Leadership

"If I had to pick one principle which I believe is key to success and critical to leadership, it would be the idea that one individual can make a difference. To be a successful leader requires, deep down, a belief that what you are doing is important, and that you can and will make a difference in people's lives by pursuing your ideals and your goals. Leadership, to me, reflects a commitment to a cause, and a determination to convince others that the cause is important."

...Senator Joseph R. Biden, Jr., Delaware

"Leadership requires inspiration, perspiration, and a determination to stand on principle even when it may be uncomfortable to do so."

...Senator Jesse Helms, North Carolina

"I believe education, hard work, determination and previous experience help to prepare individuals for leadership...The more difficult the decision, the more I knew it was important to remain true to my beliefs, my instincts and my values."

...Senator Richard Shelby, Alabama

"I believe that leadership is composed of two basic elements — knowing what is right in terms of what

26

direction the country needs to move in, and knowing how to persuade people to follow you in that direction. Unfortunately, some politicians today practice a brand of "leadership" which is actually its opposite: they follow public opinion based on what the polls tell them the people want."

...Senator Paul D. Coverdell, Georgia

"Leadership is so complex that it almost defies a simple definition. It is many values rolled into one. A strong leader must not only be a visionary, he or she must have organizational skills and the personal temperament to translate the goal into reality."

...Senator Orrin G. Hatch, Utah

On Great Leaders in American History

"Early in our nation's history, we were blessed with leaders of uncommon vision and courage who were willing to sacrifice short-term comforts for long-term gain. I think of General George Washington at Valley Forge, whose moral strength brought the American army through hardship and onto victory when all around him were ready to abandon the cause. But most of all I think of Thomas Jefferson, who believed passionately that the American experiment in self-government could survive only if Americans remained self-reliant and their government remained limited."

...Senator Paul D. Coverdell, Georgia

"Certainly many of our Founding Fathers — committed to the belief that liberty, equality, and fundamental human dignity are intrinsic human rights and that government has an obligation to protect and ensure those rights — fall into that category. Thomas Jefferson certainly comes to mind, along with George Washington and John Adams.

President Abraham Lincoln, firm in his belief that the Union must be preserved and confident in his ability to bring a fractured nation back together, certainly exemplified those qualities. Similarly, President Franklin Roosevelt's faith in the strength of the American spirit and his ability to restore Americans' faith in themselves qualifies him as a great leader at a time when leadership was so sorely needed."

...Senator Joseph R. Biden, Jr., Delaware

"Throughout our history, our nation has been blessed with many strong, multidimensional leaders, starting with the Revolutionary War period. One cannot, for example, overstate the importance of George Washington's leadership skills either as the commander of a rag tag group of revolutionary militia or as the first, precedent-setting president. Failure at the first task clearly would have meant defeat for the colonies and certain death for all of our other extraordinary Founding Fathers. Failure at the second would have produced so much instability in the fledgling American government that the United States could have found itself easy prey for stronger European nations or for a second revolution from within. Washington possessed a clear vision for the presidency, and he

*conducted the affairs of our nation with an impressive
ability both to persuade and negotiate."*
...Senator Orrin G. Hatch, Utah

On America's Rise to Greatness

*"Those leaders, determined in their vision and
confident in their cause, have helped to make America the
great nation that it is. And the fact that nature has blessed
us with many natural resources has also contributed to
America's greatness. But I believe that the true foundation
of our nation's greatness lies deep within the character of
the American people. Americans are a tough, resilient,
compassionate, forward-thinking people who place a great
value upon freedom and fundamental fairness allowing
each individual the opportunity to pursue their dreams. It
is those qualities which I believe have, for more than two
centuries, allowed this nation to rise to greatness."*
...Senator Joseph R. Biden, Jr., Delaware

*"I think the key to America's greatness is its people —
a free people. It was the genius of our Founding Fathers
to understand that a limited government was one which
would maximize the freedom and opportunity of the
American people to achieve great things. Again, Thomas
Jefferson (in his inaugural address) said it best: 'A wise
and frugal government, which shall restrain men from
injuring one another, shall leave them otherwise free to*

29

regulate their own pursuits of industry and improvement, and shall not take from the mouths of labor the bread it has earned.' At the same time, America is great also because its people are generous — generous towards our fellow Americans in need, and towards those around the world who owe their freedom today to the sacrifices of young American soldiers throughout this century."

...Senator Paul D. Coverdell, Georgia

"There is no question in my mind — and Benjamin Franklin made it clear at Philadelphia at the time this country was created — God blessed this nation in such a remarkable way..."

...Senator Jesse Helms, North Carolina

"America became a great nation for several reasons. First, given a colonial economy that was 'land rich and labor poor,' Americans have always worked hard. Second, Americans have always been innovative. A system of free enterprise, in which one may keep the rewards of hard work and better ideas, has contributed to America's growth as a prosperous, industrial power. Third, Americans have learned to blend many cultures into one melting pot. Our immigrant heritage has woven a strong fabric. Nations that have failed to assimilate other cultures find themselves beset by fractiousness and disorder. This is why I believe we must root out intentional discrimination of any kind.

Last, I agree with the 19th century French political observer Alexis de Tocqueville who said America is great because it is good. Americans, though driving for individual success, have always risen to the aid of those less fortunate. Communities have always rallied when there is trouble or disaster. Churches, charities of various types, and a vast network of volunteers still provide the backbone of our social service system. As citizens, we must not fail to support them."

...Senator Orrin G. Hatch, Utah

This book discusses the uniqueness of American success among the world's great nations, and how the leadership attributes of vision, courage, perseverance, responsibility, and character have played a key role in that success. I have drawn on the lives of five of our Founding Fathers to help illustrate these qualities. As is true with all leaders, each one of these individuals could have been used to illustrate any of the elements of leadership. Additionally, each one of the men who I use to demonstrate great leadership is not without faults. However, I believe that one of the key elements that marks us as human beings and that defines our character and responsibility is the ability to deal forthrightly with our mistakes and move forward.

Chapter One

Our American Journey

"So then, to every man his chance — to every man,
regardless of his birth; his shining, golden opportunity — to
every man the right to live, to work, to be himself,
and to become whatever thing his manhood and his vision
can combine to make him — this seeker, is the
promise of America."
– Thomas Wolfe

Today, America stands alone at the pinnacle. The Cold War, that greatest, most dangerous war of all time, is over. We have won. Neutral nations and Third World countries that once raged in anger against us, burned our flag, and marched in the streets in front of our embassies are now revisiting the American experience. It is as if they have picked up the conversation where they left off in the 1950s. "What is America all about? What were you saying? Tell us about yourself. Explain the last 45 years. What does it mean?"

Communism, that very seductive intellectual exercise, is on the trash heap. Scholars and politicians who once urged an accommodation with communism out of fear or maybe even out of genuine idealism now wince with embarrassment when the word is spoken in public. But it is hardly spoken at all, publicly or privately. Discredited by its own, the whole idea of communism is being deeply repressed by the human psyche.

The Cold War victory marks the culmination of a remarkable century of American ascendancy. But America was not always big, not always rich, not always the most powerful nation on earth.

"Do what you can, with what you have, where you are." – *Theodore Roosevelt*

In the late eighteenth century, the United States had a population of less than five million people. France and Britain were the world's super powers. Both the French and British Empires had populations close to 28 million. The British Isles alone had a population three times that of America, and their Empire would double in size near the end of the century. If France and Britain were the powers to be reckoned with, the Spanish Empire was even larger in size. The Dutch East Indies (today's Indonesia), then with a population of 12 million people, and rich in spices, was considered a land with much more abundant resources than the United States. The vulnerable, often subjugated, state of Poland had twice the American population and was arguably twice as important politically. The Japanese, considered today to be America's greatest economic rival, had six times as many people.

In 1803, with the stroke of a pen, the United States doubled in size. To finance his war with Europe, Napoleon sold the Louisiana Territory to the United States. The land stretched from the Gulf of Mexico to the Canadian border. The purchase gave the country the mighty Mississippi

River, and overnight, the new American city of New Orleans became the largest city in our young Republic.

Within one generation, the central plains of the United States became the breadbasket of the new country, and in a nine-year-period, the city of Chicago grew from a settlement of 200 to become the largest grain market in the world.

American inventiveness was born with the country and has never stopped growing. Benjamin Franklin developed the lightning rod in 1752. It was the beginning of an understanding of how electrical energy could be harnessed. About a century later, Thomas Edison invented the light bulb and the phonograph, bringing sound, as well as light to the night. In 1807, Robert Fulton built the world's first steamboat and in 1837, Samuel Morse made the world a smaller place by introducing the telegraph. In 1903, the Wright brothers flew a heavier than air, motorized airplane, and incredibly, just over sixty years later, Neil Armstrong set foot on the moon. In 1944, Howard Hathaway Aiken inaugurated the information age by building the world's first computer.

The Worker's Paradise

Ironically, America has become the very worker's paradise that Karl Marx once envisioned for socialism and communism. Economic figures are easy to juggle but no numbers can hide the purchasing power of the average American worker. For example, Sweden will show very competitive numbers for the average wage of its workers, but just go shopping in Sweden and see how much you can buy with your money. In the wealthy nations of the West, taxes and shipping costs drive the price of consumer goods through the roof. Europeans wandering through a *Sam's Warehouse* in the United States are flabbergasted by the low prices.

In this country there are two working radios for every man, woman, boy, girl, and infant. I say, "working radios" because Americans literally throw their radios in the trash when they break down. Moreover, there is nearly one television set per capita. Much is made of America's economic rivalry with Japan and the rise of the Japanese auto industry, but American highways carry five times as many motor vehicles as its nearest rival. By 1996, there were, in fact, almost as many registered motor vehicles in the United States as there were people, almost twice the per capita total of Japan. America has six times the railroad miles of its mother country, the United Kingdom, which is famous for its railroads. Additionally, America has ten times the number of automobiles.

America owns 85% of the world's computers, manufactures 75% of the world's aircraft, and 65% of its pharmaceuticals. It is by any measure the communications center of the world. The United States, together with the United Kingdom, Australia and Canada, are probably the only countries in the world where the media is not routinely suborned by government or business. Our military might is now unrivaled, and for the moment anyway, we are at the pinnacle. Or so it seems.

Who Gets the Glory?

There are many theories about America's rise to greatness. One rather entertaining idea advanced by some French historians lays it all at the feet of the French. Not only did they step in to defend America's pitiful army in its War of Independence, but two decades later they gave up the vast Louisiana Territory. It was Napoleon Bonaparte's ill-advised adventurous European wars that built America, the French historians reason. The wars bankrupted the French Empire, forcing the sale of Louisiana. Into the vacuum of Napoleon's "failure of excess" stepped the ubiquitous British who ruled the world for a hundred years. An Anglo-American dominance has been in play ever since. That is how many French students of history see us. And there is some truth in their perspective.

However, while France did play a pivotal role in the birth of our nation, a case can be made that she benefited as much as we by her involvement in the American Revolution. Her small forces were able to tie down a much larger British Royal Expeditionary Force and fleet, keeping them far from the European theater of affairs for a very long time. France can certainly take no credit for the great American industrial awakening, nor its inventiveness in the 19th century. And as if to even the score, twice during this century United States forces played a leading role in liberating France from her German invaders, first in 1917 during WWI, and again in 1944 on D-Day.

Other historians, most of them from the United Kingdom, credit America's success specifically to the British navy. Their warships ruled the seas, protected world trade, and allowed American trade to flourish for a hundred years without America having to carry any of the financial burden. In an attempt to recruit us to their version of history, they liken it to our role in the latter half of the 20th century. The United States spent billions of dollars to develop weapons, police the world, protect our allies and neutral nations from the Soviets, while the economies of Japan and Germany flourished, spending relatively nothing on their own defense.

The British claim that they could have won the so-called War of Independence. They were bigger, stronger, and had defeated more resourceful opponents. They simply decided that it wasn't worth it. That is how many English students of history see us, and there is some truth to this perspective as well.

While the British navy of the 19th century did indeed protect the world's sea lanes, America was not the only nation to benefit. Indeed, if that were the preeminent secret to America's greatness, then Canada would surely be the world's greatest economic powerhouse. She was Britain's favorite child. Her four million square miles of abundant resources surpassed continental America's three million square miles. By contrast, while America sometimes benefited from her British cousins, she was also punished by two British wars. In 1814 English soldiers occupied Washington, D. C. and burned the White House to the ground.

Most non-Americans see our success as an accident of geography. America had timber, fertile soil, and vast mineral wealth to lure the people inland. Certainly, this country's vast natural resources have played their part in our success. That perspective is also valid.

However, the claim that America's greatness is simply a product of her natural resources is untrue. By such standards, South Africa, Australia, and Brazil would all be super powers, and the Soviet Union would have trounced the United States in the Cold War. In fact, anyone who has ever taken a transcontinental flight across North America is amazed by the thousands of miles of unusable land. Fully one-third of America is too cold to sustain productive agriculture and one-fourth is virtually either unusable desert or uninhabitable mountains.

"The fate of America cannot depend on any one man. The greatness of America is grounded in principles and not on any single personality."
– Franklin D. Roosevelt

Most Americans see themselves and their culture as the secret to their success. It is our character, we like to believe. No matter how cynical and self-critical we have become, this is what we must still truly believe because this is what we still teach our children. It is what we ourselves learned in our early school years. It is the people who made this country great.

But if it is the people who made it great, why did they not make their own lands great? Why did these British, Irish, German, Italian, and African immigrants and slaves suddenly become inventive and industrious on this side of the Atlantic? Why didn't they build their own countries into world powers? Why come here to do it?

Well, it was the "melting pot," and the mongrel is smarter than the pedigree. Perhaps there is some truth in this perspective as well. Most Americans are familiar with the moving words of Emma Lazarus, inscribed on the base of the Statue of Liberty: "Give me your tired, your poor, your huddled masses yearning to breathe free." Very few notice the next line, "The wretched *refuse* of your teeming shore." Give me the wretched refuse?

In fact, Lazarus was fairly accurate, for that is what we are: the refuse, the garbage of the world. We are the poor, the powerless, the oppressed, the weakest of society. We are the Puritans fleeing from England, seeking a place to worship, or the Baptist Huguenots fleeing France and Spain. We are the Catholics fleeing England, forming colonies in the Carolinas. We were not the wealthy, the strong, or the influential. Usually the powerful stayed behind. They could buy their freedoms. We are the Africans who were caught or betrayed into slavery. We are the starving Irish who came in the midst of the Potato Famine. We are the Jews fleeing Czarist Russia and later Hitler's Germany. We are the Italians who started coming in great numbers after the Economic Panic of 1879. We are the Vietnamese boat people, coming by the hundreds of thousands in the 1970s. Today, we are the Hispanics crossing the borders of Texas and California. Yet we, the garbage of the world, "the refuse," have built the greatest nation on earth.

The American Way

Most students would contend that all of these factors played their part in the evolution of American greatness, but there was indeed something else, an intangible, spiritual influence. There was a common philosophy that bound the Founding Fathers and early frontiersmen. It was a philosophy born out of the decision to come to the New World in the first place and a philosophy forged out of common experiences of isolation and early danger and deprivation. Some argue that the 19th century American age of inventiveness sprang right from the soil of independent frontiersmen and pioneer women who, after waiting three months for a ship to bring the right tool or piece of cloth, and another three months to get it through the inhospitable land, learned to find solutions on their own. Independent, with self-initiative, they soon learned to be resourceful or they died. America became a nation of leaders. Small wonder that she would one day lead other nations.

"Leaders are the custodians of a nation's ideals, of the beliefs it cherishes, of its permanent hopes, of the faith which makes a nation out of a mere aggregation of individuals." – Walter Lippmann

---

Thus, this wonderful cauldron of events and people not only gave birth to a new nation, it gave birth to a prescription for living. It is this philosophy, this American "spirit," which we will explore in this first volume introducing the American Leadership Foundation. Discussed here are five principles, exemplified by the lives of early American heroes. Woven throughout their stories are the principles that have made America a great nation, principles that have worked collectively for us as a nation and which can work individually for anyone who will dare to employ them for themselves.

Chapter Two

Benjamin Franklin - Power of Vision

"The rapid progress true science now makes, occasions my regretting sometimes that I was born so soon."
– Benjamin Franklin

Anthropologists have long observed that every society has unique characteristics. For the American, nothing is more distinctive than his or her inventiveness, imagination, or what some have called "American know-how." I am not referring here solely to engineering, such as the Wright brothers and their flying machine, but also to the wealth of ideas that have revolutionized industry, education, and the role of government. There is Henry Ford's immensely practical concept of an assembly line, or Charles Birdseye's development of frozen food. Innovations run the gamut from mundane conveniences such as self-service supermarkets, fast-food restaurants, and shopping malls, to today's exploding communication marvel, the world wide web, initiated and still today dominated by American subscribers.

People of the world often complain about the dominance of American ideas, and even many Americans bemoan the blurring of rich cultural and national distinctions. Some governments pass laws to resist the impact. The French, for example, limit the number of American movies on French television. But nothing can stop the flow. The French may still champion *haute cuisine* but the masses of the world are eating American pizza and McDonald's french fries. The youth of the world from Jakarta to Budapest are watching *MTV* while their little brothers and sisters are entertained by Disney videos. Their parents, meanwhile, enjoy their own cultural and linguistic versions of the American game *Wheel of Fortune*.

In most cases it is the simple equation of supply and demand at work, which is all too often ignored by other industrial nations who expect that it is their "right" to coerce consumers into buying into their own homegrown culture. At other times, an American concept is only an obvious solution to a modern problem (fast food, for example). But the truly remarkable fact is that this phenomenon has been at work for two hundred years. Americans seem to come equipped with the ability to change the environment, to build, to discover, to adapt, and to see things that others can't see.

"The problems of the world cannot possibly be solved by skeptics or cynics whose horizons are limited by the obvious realities. We need men who can dream of things that never were."
– John F. Kennedy

Anton Signorile, noted Italian historian, suggests that vision is a trait born in the immigrants even before they arrive in America. In fact, the type of person drawn to

America is already a "dreamer." Indeed, since Christopher Columbus, the vision of America has fired the imagination of the world. America has been different things for different people at different times in history. In the midst of the Potato Famine, Irish fathers would describe a bountiful land with rich soil, and a vast ocean moat to keep out the blight that continually ruined their crops. Italian shepherds, crowded by the mountains on one side and the sea on the other, were told of millions of hectares of abundant grasslands. Jews in Czarist Russia could describe a land of religious and cultural freedom, where one could openly be a Jew without persecution. Steven Speilberg captured the mood in his cartoon feature *An American Tail*. The mice all sing lustily, "there are no cats in America."

Of course, there are indeed cats in America, as Speilberg's mice were to discover. Nor did many of the Italians ever reach the abundant grasslands or the Irish plow the fertile soil. Most of them never got out of the city. The Jews found that the virus of bigotry had already taken root in the New World. Nevertheless, no setback, no heavy dose of reality seemed to shake the mythology of America or the dream and the optimism that the immigrants brought with them. Having created the ideal in their own minds they stubbornly set about trying to make it happen. It is a process that continues to this day.

There is great debate about whether America has ever lived up to the myth, but it is a moot point. No one doubts that by any measure, she has succeeded abundantly simply by trying. Many credit President Ronald Reagan's threat to build the new Star Wars defense technology as the final

49

nail in the coffin of the Soviet Empire and the final factor in ending the Cold War. Many scientists openly ridiculed the feasibility of such a project but the world had seen the Americans do the impossible too many times before. Mikhail Gorbachev decided he couldn't take that chance. Once more, the American myth triumphed.

The Writings of "Silence Do Good"

Perhaps no other figure in American history so embodies the spirit of creativity and resourcefulness as does Benjamin Franklin. Inventor, writer, humorist, diplomat, Franklin was for years America's most popular and creative public persona. Most historians venture, that had he been born a few years later, he would surely have been one of America's first presidents.

Benjamin Franklin was born into a poor New England family on January 17, 1706. He was the 15th child of Josiah Franklin. His mother, Abiah Folger, was Josiah's second wife. At age thirteen, Franklin was apprenticed to his brother James who had just returned from England with a new printing press. While learning the trade of a printer, Franklin devoured the many books that were then accessible. It was not so much the quantity of books that distinguished Franklin's private studies as his concentration on the style of prose and the underlying philosophy of the author. Franklin committed huge portions of his favorite literary works to memory, including John Bunyan's classic,

Pilgrim's Progress, and Sir Richard Steele's third volume of the *Spectator*. It was a type of concentrated study that became his habit and it followed him the rest of his life.

In 1721, Benjamin's brother, James, launched a newspaper called the *New England Courant*. Young Ben set the type, ran the presses, and delivered the papers. When he tried submitting articles of his own however, he was rejected sternly by his older brother. And so was eventually born the legend of "Silence Do Good," the anonymous sage of Boston. Stung by the rejection of his older brother, Benjamin began submitting anonymous articles to the newspaper. His anonymous essays provoked such discussion that Franklin soon began a more ambitious project. Privately publishing under the pseudonym of a New England matriarch named Silence Do Good, Benjamin Franklin began to take the colonial establishment to task. No subject was too sacred for Mrs. Do Good's sarcasm and biting wit. Colonial officials and powerful religious leaders were often infuriated by the criticism and ridicule, but the wider public was delighted. Boston was abuzz with the audacity and humor of the mysterious writer.

With time, James Franklin caught on and Benjamin's moonlighting career as Boston sage was exposed. Most of James' friends were amazed that for months a fifteen-year-old had charmed the reading public of the whole city. Preachers had been debating his ideas from the pulpit; politicians had been searching for his irreverent, between-the-lines humor, and the general public had been waiting anxiously for each new installment. Nevertheless, James, the serious, hard-working brother was not amused. Failing totally to appreciate the abundant talent in one so young, he canceled the column and ordered Benjamin back to setting type. Failing to win the respect of his own brother, Benjamin finally left, making his way to Philadelphia where he soon found work in another print shop.

In Philadelphia, a thriving marketing town with a population of 5000, young Benjamin seemed to have finally found the support he needed. Sir William Keith, the provisional governor of Pennsylvania was taken by the young printer. Using his old trick from Boston, Franklin managed to get some of his articles printed anonymously. Keith saw how such words moved the public and provoked the city fathers. Franklin's wit and remarkable knowledge convinced Keith that he would be a good investment politically, as well as financially. Promising letters of credit and introduction, Keith persuaded Franklin to sail to London to buy the printing presses needed to launch his own business in Philadelphia. But Keith's promises were empty. At eighteen years of age, Benjamin Franklin found himself alone and penniless in a foreign city, abandoned by his promised benefactor.

A natural optimist, Franklin did not have time to feel sorry for himself. Using his wit and demonstrating his command of the printing business, he soon found employment with the most prestigious printing firm in England. Before the year was over, young Benjamin Franklin was corresponding and meeting with the most distinguished literary and publishing figures in Great Britain. The self-educated, uniquely American Benjamin Franklin, was an enigmatic, youthful curiosity to the traditional, staid world of English writing and publishing, where every line and idea could be anticipated. Though still quite young, Franklin was accepted by many of his new acquaintances as both a provocative conversationalist and a gentleman.

Poor Richard's Almanac

In 1726, Benjamin Franklin was welcomed back to his beloved Philadelphia. The former provisional governor, Sir William Keith, who had abandoned him in London now offered him new work as if nothing had happened. Franklin accepted, but having learned his lesson, he simultaneously began seeking alternatives.

That summer, Franklin brought together a number of distinguished young Philadelphians into a discussion group which called itself the Junto Club. In time it would become the American Philosophical Society. By 1730, with financial backing from fellow members of the club, Benjamin Franklin finally bought his own printing press and launched the *Pennsylvania Gazette*. It was an immediate success. Franklin was twenty-four-years-old.

Typically, Benjamin Franklin used his press to generate business. After receiving a modest contract to print money, he circulated an anonymous tract extolling the economic virtues of expanding the money supply. Young Franklin's anonymous paper stirred up a lively public debate which earned him even more money printing contracts and prompted numerous follow-up essays, this time on the public record. Before the decade was over, Franklin's tracts on the money supply, whatever their original purpose, were read and discussed all across Europe and attracted the attention of both Karl Marx and economist Adam Smith.

In 1732, he began publishing a farmer's almanac under the pen name of Richard Saunders. Within a few short years *Poor Richard's Almanac* became an annual best seller in all thirteen colonies, loved even more for its political satire and homespun wisdom than its weather forecasts and calendar of events. In most homes of the primitive and rugged American frontier, the Bible and *Poor Richard's Almanac* were the only reading materials available. Youngsters were taught how to read with the *Almanac* as the primer. Franklin's philosophical musings had a pervasive influence on the personality of the young colonies. "A penny saved is a penny earned," wrote Franklin. Over time, debates raged on whether such favorite verses were from the Bible or Franklin's *Almanac*.

During his early years, Franklin seemed to be constantly on the brink of financial ruin. While there was still no evidence that his spreading notoriety and famous friends would ever translate into financial security, he nonetheless now felt confident enough to ask a longtime Philadelphia friend for her hand in marriage. On September 1, 1730, Benjamin Franklin and Miss Deborah Read were married in Philadelphia. They had two children, a boy who died at the age of four and Sarah Franklin, who later became Mrs. Richard Bache.

Franklin was 30 years old when he was drafted to run for clerk of the Pennsylvania General Assembly. The city fathers, who saw much talent in the young Franklin, made sure that he had no opposition. Before the year was out, Colonel Spotswood, Postmaster General of Philadelphia, appointed Franklin as his deputy, adding yet another modest salary to Franklin's growing sources of revenue.

Man of Science

It was not Benjamin Franklin's writings, however, nor his modest political activities that first earned him fame abroad. From adolescence onward Franklin became a well-spring of ideas and inventions. "Look around you," he would urge his fellow Junto members, "the solution to most problems is right before our eyes." He was a true visionary, never satisfied with the status quo. In Philadelphia, Franklin conceived of a modern city municipal system with a police force paid by a modest tax on property owners. He organized a citywide volunteer fire department. He launched an academy for the "complete education of youth," which eventually grew to become the University of Pennsylvania. He convinced fellow Junto Club members to donate books into a common pool which would, in turn, "lend" those books to the community. It became the first modern, public library in the American colonies. He founded the first hospital in America and published its first medical books. His printing press published the first American novel.

His inquiring mind, energized by his confidence in material progress, made him a true figure of "The

Enlightenment." Nothing so engrossed him as the manifestations of nature. Because of the advances of 18th century science, as well as the exacting techniques of experimental observation, nature was no longer regarded as mystical. Franklin's curiosity ranged from the causes of earthquakes and the benefits of the Gulf Stream for navigation, to the possible association of lightning and electricity, culminating in his famous kite-and-key experiment. His *Experiments and Observations on Electricity* (1753) brought him international fame as one of the leading scientific figures of his day.

At the same time, there was a common theme running throughout most of Franklin's innovations and discoveries. It was always something practical, and in retrospect, always something that should have been obvious. Sitting before a fireplace one night, Franklin mused about the fact that all the warmth was escaping through the chimney. Before the week was up he had redesigned the fireplace, and within another month had perfected the "Franklin Stove."

Franklin the Statesman

As a result of his reputation, the colonial government would call on Franklin throughout his life to help solve a crisis. During the French and Indian War, he was asked to organize the defenses of Philadelphia. In 1757, he was sent to England by the Pennsylvania Assembly to plead their case before the King. In this instance, proprietary lands granted to the founding colonial family of William

Penn were tax exempt and had become a drain on the growing local governments. As usual, Franklin charmed his hosts and was soon the talk of London. As a favorite dinner guest, Franklin could regale his listeners with tales of Indian savages or quote long passages of Shakespeare.

England did not intimidate Franklin in the least. A bright mind and a quick study, he seemed to be equally at home in Oxford or on the American frontier. While in the United Kingdom, Franklin conceived of new methods for paving streets. He also developed new designs for street lamps that would allow them to burn longer and brighter. His experimentation with colors sparked new scientific debate and thrilled the English public. By placing various pieces of cloth in the snow, Franklin learned that the darker colors absorbed the heat and melted the snow, while white reflected the sunlight. Fashion was forever changed.

During his eleven years in Great Britain, tension between the colonies and the mother country increased. Franklin worked tirelessly to avoid a showdown. When American riots broke out over the so-called Stamp Act, Franklin was called before Parliament where he spoke for four hours answering more than 170 questions, and left some of England's best and brightest amazed at his wisdom and political skill. The following week the English Parliament canceled the hated Stamp Act and Benjamin Franklin was hailed a hero across the American colonies.

Still, no compromise could avert war. In Boston, a playful snowball fight between colonists and British soldiers ended in a riot with four colonists shot to death. When a colonial governor called for more English troops, suggesting that the colonies were enjoying too much liberty,

Franklin leaked the letters which incited more riots and prompted an enraged Parliament to issue a summons. With memories of his last appearance, Benjamin Franklin left for Parliament full of hope for a resolution to the crisis. Instead, Franklin was ridiculed personally and attacked viciously. Members of Parliament heaped upon him all of their frustration and anger with the restless American colonies. He uttered not a word and left silently, a reluctant revolutionary. Many British statesmen would soon regret losing their most effective link to the American people and gaining their most enterprising adversary.

Sorrowfully, Benjamin Franklin bid farewell to his few loyal English friends and sailed home to the colonies. By the time he reached Philadelphia, the battles of Concord and Lexington had already been fought and blood had been shed.

The emerging young nation needed all the help it could get and Benjamin Franklin's experience and talents were put to immediate use. He was elected to the Second Continental Congress, chosen to serve on ten of its committees, was named the postmaster general for the new nation and was one of five men called on to write the Declaration of Independence. When that famous document was finally signed, John Hancock made the wry comment that they had better "win this war" or they would all hang together. Whereupon Franklin quipped, "We must surely hang together or we will most certainly hang separately."

Defying the British Crown was serious business. The Empire rivaled France as the most powerful nation on earth, with the British navy giving it a crucial edge. Since sailing ships required winds to take them across the vast oceans, they could only travel on the same routes back and forth across the seas. Most critical of all were the narrow straits or "doorways" that linked the various sea lanes and opened the way from one ocean to another. With a small number of soldiers, a carefully placed fort, a few cannons, and the guarantee of ships to offer resupply, a British force could hold such a position indefinitely. For almost three generations the British had been seizing such strategic points, giving them a virtual power lock on world trade. Even more importantly, the British knew how to leverage such power to political advantage.

The consensus was that the American colonies would be isolated and doomed to defeat even before their effort began. Their only hope lay in gaining financial and military assistance from a British rival strong enough and angry enough to thumb its nose at British power.

From the beginning, there had really been only one possibility for American independence and that was with help from France. The court of Versailles under Louis XVI and Marie Antoinette was at the pinnacle of its splendor and corruption. For four generations France had been the foremost land power on the continent, leaving its crowned heads time and money to pursue any and every extravagance. But the wealth of the nation had been plundered by three successive, extravagant kings. In fact, the Bank of France was in a very dangerous state. The people were suffering. The French Revolution, which would have a cataclysmic impact on the world, was only a few years away. The government of Louis XVI had no business taking on an expensive and politically risky client state.

Nevertheless, Benjamin Franklin, the famous and endearing American, took France by storm. From the day he arrived, his every move was followed with delight and praise. When Franklin arrived wearing a fur cap instead of a wig, the fact was duly noted by journalists and fur caps starting appearing all over the streets of Paris. His favorite restaurants were packed with customers. Renowned scientists and philosophers flocked to see him and discuss his theories on electricity or his radical concepts on personal liberty. Socially, he was a huge success, entertained almost nightly by the greatest social mavens in Paris. The very qualities that had sometimes made him suspect to his American critics seemed to endear him to the French. His flirtations with the opposite sex, his controversial theological views, his irreverent and sly wit with its *double-entendre*, all served him well with his French hosts.

By the time he was finally brought to the court at Versailles, Franklin had much of the nation behind him. Common folk and the disgruntled masses identified with this ambassador of downtrodden, revolutionary America. The nobility and friends of the King were totally smitten. And the court's advisors felt that arming the Americans was cheaper and more effective than an outright war with England. Louis finally agreed to the arms Franklin requested and eventually advanced the six million dollars to pay for them. It was a fateful decision both for the American revolutionaries and the French court. Historians still debate whether this drain on the dwindling French treasury was the final nail in the coffin for the court at Versailles.

Man of Controversy

On the other hand, Benjamin Franklin was not without detractors. Perhaps no other Founding Father was so controversial. In his early career as a pamphleteer he engaged in a running feud with George Whitfield, the foremost preacher of his day. Young Franklin's penchant for paraphrasing scripture and then declaring his version better than the original struck many devout New Englanders as arrogant and blasphemous. His experiments with lightning were likewise offensive to churchmen on three continents, who warned that lightning was God's weapon for punishing sinful men and Franklin's attempt to harness it was sacrilegious.

Franklin's finances initiated frequent controversy, with accusations of profiteering and benefiting from insider government contracts. He placed printing presses in most of the major cities in the thirteen colonies and soon cornered the market on paper, thus profiting from his competitors as well. The expenses involved in his mission to France were hotly debated back home, but final audits showed nothing amiss.

Unquestionably, the greatest concern about Benjamin Franklin was his reputation as a womanizer, and not only the pious were shocked. The great British writer D. H. Lawrence declared him a "hypocrite and a fraud," a man who peddled middle-class morality but lived like a hedonist. Future president John Adams and his wife, who later accompanied Franklin to Paris, were stunned at his comportment with the women of France. "Women the age of his grandchildren, shamelessly threw themselves at him and he exploited every opportunity to its fullest," said Adams.

Franklin's first child, William, was born out of wedlock, an admitted indiscretion with a "wanton woman." He and his wife, Deborah Read, became married only through common law. For historians, the greatest treasure-trove of Franklin correspondence is his love letters to beautiful women of England and France, correspondence which he continued till the day he died. In his latter years, when Deborah had finally died, Benjamin Franklin's relationship with a young, wealthy, married French lady became the grist of scandalous international gossip, though Franklin's own correspondence reveals that the relationship was never consummated.

Controversies notwithstanding, Benjamin Franklin was probably the greatest American of his age. He was certainly the most famous. Franklin's face adorned plates, coins, scarfs, medallions and made such items best-sellers. He was the foremost scientist of his generation, an Einstein called forth to be a statesman. In the end, Franklin's homespun wisdom and wit endeared him to so many that his faults were forgiven by the masses and perversely applauded by sophisticates, especially the French.

In 1785, at seventy-nine years of age, Benjamin Franklin persuaded his government to let him return to his beloved, new United States to die. Pithy to the end, Franklin remarked on his death bed, "Only two things are certain in life, taxes and death."

Many great, younger Americans followed him into history — George Washington, Thomas Jefferson, John Adams — but while he lived, Franklin's fame towered above them all as one of our most important Founding Fathers. Whether viewed as a philosopher, a scientist, or a statesman, Benjamin Franklin's career is illustrative of the power of vision. Ideas and speculative thinking must ultimately be translated into actions and objects. Franklin was not content merely to demonstrate that lightning was electrical energy; he invented the battery to store it. This kind of pragmatism and resourcefulness has become an essential ingredient of the American character. Europeans — Einstein, Bohr, Rutherford — developed the theory leading to the discovery of atomic energy. It took the determination and resourcefulness of a General Groves and a Dr. Robert Oppenheimer to transform the theoretical vision of nuclear reaction into the bombs that were dropped upon Hiroshima and Nagasaki that ended WWII. Later, that vision was put to good use in peacetime reactors that supply clean, abundant, and economical electrical energy to most of Western Europe and parts of the United States.

VISION

> *"Cherish your visions and your dreams as they are the children of your soul; the blue prints of your ultimate achievements."*
> *– Napoleon Hill*

One of the most wonderful things that we have is the ability to dream. We can become what we want to become in a nation that was built on the wings of a dream. This is the principle that gives flight to all of America's great success stories.

The first step to any success is to see it, to visualize it. It is a principle as old as the Bible which proclaims that "without a vision the people perish." Whether you are in search of a happy marriage or a successful job it is imperative that you see this in your mind's eye. Act it out in your mind. You must rehearse your success.

Many people dismiss this as an exaggeration. They say that it is a waste of time, that it is unproductive. However, I would contend that those people making that claim have never achieved any real success nor have they ever been effective leaders. The irony is that many people will listen to them simply because it is easy to do so and seemingly exempts them from personal responsibility. The truth is quite different. Study the great leaders in America and the power of vision will prove itself.

Olympic athletes can often be found before an event with their eyes closed scoring a perfect 10 on the balance beam, or being the first to break the tape in the marathon. They are taught that their success will be a result of that which they first see happening. Great musicians can close their eyes and feel the music before a note is actually played. Military strategists foresee their opponents' movements played out on computer models before making a decision to follow a certain course of action. There is medical evidence to indicate that people can change their health status through visualization. Companies discuss the impact their decisions will have in the competitive marketplace before implementing them.

"A man may die, nations may rise and fall, but an idea lives on. Ideas have endurance without death."
– John F. Kennedy

While we used Benjamin Franklin's story to underline America's capacity to dream, it is an identifiable characteristic of almost all great Americans. Jefferson dreamed and wrote about a democratic nation, functioning far into the future. His essays anticipated many of the problems that did indeed surface in future generations. Henry Ford envisioned an affordable automobile for the masses, a totally absurd idea at the time. Walt Disney dreamed of his "magic kingdom," while Bill Gates preached the wonders of the Internet. Never forget, it was an American who said, "That's one small step for man. One giant leap for mankind," while standing on the surface of a heavenly body which dreamers gazed at nightly.

While all of us suffer under some handicap — racial or religious bigotry, lack of resources, inadequate education, physical disability — none can limit our ability to think. It is only the poverty of our dreams that holds us back from taking this important first step.

> *"Like small creeks that grow into mighty rivers, the dreams of leaders eventually shape the course of history."*
> *— Author Unknown*

Chapter Three

John Hancock - Man of Courage

"...being with one mind resolved to die free men rather than to live as slaves." – John Hancock

From the beginning, the citizens of this new land prided themselves as "the land of the free and the home of the brave." Alistair Cooke and other historians write about the "courageous" American immigrants, the type of people who would strike out and leave everything familiar and known for only a dream. While having an active imagination or vision was the inspiration, courage and boldness were necessary to get the feet moving. The fact is, Americans were visionaries and they were courageous even before they arrived on these shores. In that sense, the foundation of the American personality was set in England, France, Spain, or from wherever the pilgrims first hailed. Even the later immigrants from Italy, Czarist Russia, Poland, and Germany, while still drawn from the desperate, the poor and the persecuted, were people who knew how to nurture a dream and people who had the boldness to seek it.

"The battle, sir, is not to the strong alone;
it is to the vigilant, the active, the brave."
– Patrick Henry

Courage is part of the American formula and John Hancock, famous for his large, bold signature on the Declaration of Independence, exemplifies it best. King George would be able to read the signature, Hancock said, without putting on his glasses. No other single act spoke so eloquently of the American character.

A "Rich Rebel"

John Hancock was a preacher's son, born on January 12, 1736, in Braintree, Massachusetts to the Reverend John Hancock, 34, and his wife, Mary, nine years his junior. The future signatory of the Declaration of Independence was a middle child with an older sister, Mary, and a younger brother, Ebenezer. Life for the family was by no means lavish, but his father's paycheck was larger than most ministers' earnings of the time. "The Reverend," as his wife and everyone else called him, provided his family with a comfortable life on a Massachusetts farm and in time was able to purchase a slave, Jeffrey, to help with the chores.

From the time little John was born, it was apparent that he was headed for great things. Not only did he have two of the most respected people in Braintree for parents, but "the Reverend" made sure that his namesake received the best education colonial American life had to offer. Most assumed that John would become a minister like his father and grandfather before him.

In the spring of 1744, the world of John Hancock turned upside down. It would never stop spinning for the rest of his life. "The Reverend" took ill and then suddenly, with virtually no warning, died. The community was stunned. His widow was devastated. Unsure of where to go, she accepted an invitation from her husband's parents to live with them in Lexington.

"The Reverend's" esteemed father, known as "the Bishop," made every effort to make sure that his grandchildren were brought up properly. It grieved him that his only other son, Thomas, was a wealthy merchant with no desire to follow the family's ministerial tradition. It was assumed that young John would someday step into his father's footsteps and thus resume the family career that had been interrupted by the sudden death of his father.

When young John was eight years old, he and the family were invited to Boston for a summer with Uncle Thomas, "the Bishop's" merchant son. John's mother jumped at the chance to spend time in the most vibrant of colonial cities, especially with her brother and sister-in-law, Thomas and Lydia Hancock, two of the most wealthy and successful citizens of the town. Young John Hancock packed his things, said good-bye to his grandfather and left Lexington to visit with his uncle and aunt on Beacon Hill, never expecting that the move would be permanent.

At the time of John's move, Boston was a worldly and successful city with a dirty, urban appearance. England was in the middle of a war with Spain and France, and Boston was following the events with great seriousness. John settled into his new home quite nicely. He was given one of the largest bedrooms in the house and was waited on hand and foot by the servants and his Aunt Lydia. The impressionable lad spent much time peering out his bedroom window, watching British troops below Beacon Hill going through their drills.

Young John Hancock was in awe of his Uncle Thomas. The Hancock's of Beacon Hill entertained most of the important people of the city, as well as distinguished foreign visitors. Each day brought more information and prompted more questions. In Boston, John would hear more gossip about politics, trade and war in a day, than he had the entire year in Braintree or Lexington. The boy adjusted to his new home and the people in it without effort.

John's admiration for his uncle was returned in kind. Thomas Hancock and his wife, Lydia, were desperate for children. Thomas wanted an heir, someone prepared to follow him in his business and take his many projects and ventures even further. Thomas soon became a mentor to his young nephew.

Shortly after moving from Lexington, John was admitted to the Boston Latin School. It was here that he would gain knowledge about such subjects as history, foreign languages, philosophy, and theology. After each school day John walked several miles to the home of Mr. Abiah Holbrook to study arithmetic, writing, and spelling. It is to Abiah Holbrook that we owe John Hancock's famous penmanship.

After five years of Boston schooling, John Hancock was ready for college. In the fall of 1750, he entered Harvard University at the age of thirteen. He was one of the youngest and brightest students in his class. He was also one of the most mischievous. John was reduced four places in class ranking after he and four other sophomores visited a local tavern and got intoxicated.

Nevertheless, John Hancock managed to survive such indiscretions graduating fifth in the class of 1754. On that very day he announced to his mother that he would not be returning to Lexington. He would stay in Boston with his uncle. This was, of course, wonderful news for Uncle Thomas, the merchant. He now had an heir—someone who could build on the foundation of his burgeoning mercantile empire.

Although John was a Harvard graduate and had learned much from his uncle over the years, he was in no position to run Thomas Hancock's far flung enterprises. He stayed by Thomas's side, however, learning and helping wherever he could. By 1759, his signature began showing up on official correspondence, and in 1760, John traveled to London for business.

The trip to London turned out to be a bit more for pleasure than commerce. At his uncle's encouragement, John roamed the town, liberally spending the company's money. It was then that momentous events began to unfold. Not long after his arrival, the English King, George II, suddenly died. The obligatory mourning soon passed and the city was abuzz as the English eagerly began anticipating the coronation of the new King George III. John desperately wanted to stay for the coronation, but George III did not have a queen and finding one was going to take some time. The coronation was indefinitely postponed. Then came sad news from Boston. Lydia's father had died, and Thomas called John home before winter struck.

John Hancock returned to Boston to find his uncle in ill health. Thomas had become increasingly tired, and with John home, he felt he could ease some of his duties. Ebenezer, John's younger brother, who had also escaped the family ministerial tradition by working for his uncle, had been helping Thomas while John was away. Now, he relinquished the reins to his more experienced brother. On New Year's Day, 1763, Uncle Thomas proudly announced John's partnership in the Hancock business.

For the first few months, John single-handedly operated the business and did so quite ably, even as his Uncle Thomas's health continued to worsen. Then, in the summer of 1764, Thomas began showing signs of improvement. In fact, he was feeling so well that on the first day of August, with the encouragement of his doctors, Thomas decided to go to a council meeting. He walked in the door of the meeting room and collapsed on the floor. He was rushed home, but died a couple of hours later.

Thomas Hancock left the bulk of his estate to his wife Lydia, and his nephew John. The rest went to Harvard University for various programs, as well as to nieces, nephews, slaves, and a few close friends. Overnight, John Hancock became one of the richest men in Boston. Many a social and business maven, unfamiliar with the closeness of the relationship between uncle and nephew, was caught unaware.

No Taxation Without Representation !

The responsibility for assuming control of the Hancock mercantile business could not have come at a worse time. Great Britain was dishing out some surprising blows to the young colonies. They initiated the Sugar Act, and immediately followed with the Stamp Act. The latter was an odious and time-consuming tax, requiring a stamp on each and every written transaction including orders, bills of lading, invoices, minutes, and even personal letters. All of New England was outraged, including John Hancock. His newly acquired business began failing fast. A popular pamphleteer, James Otis, began propounding the theme of "no taxation without representation." John Hancock quickly became an outspoken supporter of the idea.

With his excellent education and newly inherited money, the suddenly politically active merchant, John Hancock, was enthusiastically voted a selectman in Boston. John immediately wrote letters to his London contacts stating that he would purposely lay up any ships arriving after the first of November. He vowed not to have "any kind of connection in business under a Stamp." When other Boston businessmen sought ways to resist the new tax, he quickly stepped forward to help organize them. Eventually, 250 merchants signed the famous nonimportation agreement. Each businessman made a public vow to cancel all imports until the revocation of the hated Stamp Act.

75

This seemingly small initiative had a profound impact. Angry British merchants now losing money from the colonies protested to Parliament. As we now know, colonial representative Benjamin Franklin was called before parliament and quizzed for hours and the English Crown quickly backed down. On April 17, 1766, it was announced that Great Britain would revoke the notorious Stamp Act. For his part in the drama, John Hancock became very popular in Boston and was soon elected one of the city's representatives.

Nonetheless, soon after the repeal of the Stamp Act, John lost all interest in Bostonian politics. His business was slipping away from him and desperately needed his attention. John put politics on the back burner and once more focused on the many and diverse enterprises of his mercantile empire. John wrote friends that the "political phase" of his life was over.

Only weeks after John's private resignation from political life, "Champagne Charlie" Townsend, Chancellor of the Exchequer for the King, suggested a selective tax for the colonies on items "specified by the Crown." Included on the infamous list was glass, painter's colors, red and white lead, paper, and tea. This act, known as the Townsend Act, also contained a clause allowing Crown officers to search and seize anyone's home, anytime they liked, in an effort to collect such duties. It passed the British Parliament without dissent.

John Hancock was reenergized. He once again initiated a nonimportation agreement, urging businesses to support local manufacturers only and agreeing not to import a long list of British products, including many of the most popular luxuries. Hancock's boldness in confronting British authorities once more galvanized the business community to action. The people of Boston cheered him on. He was reelected as a selectman and recruited to a list of other positions as well. He was appointed to several positions, including a committee formed to draft a letter of thanks to John Dickinson, author of "Letters from a Farmer in Pennsylvania to the Inhabitants of the British Colonies," written to show disgust for the Townsend Duties.

Standing Alone

The boiling resentment spreading through the colonies sometimes erupted in violence. Particularly vulnerable were the British customs commissioners who were often targeted by angry colonists. The commissioners appealed to Massachusetts Governor Bernard to send troops, but the governor refused, offering them only the use of Castle William, located in the harbor. They would be safe there, he assured them, and he would provide police assistance if needed. Seeing that they could expect little help from the governor, customs officials appealed to London for help.

In England, the Earl of Hillsborough received the complaints and took the lead in urging immediate action. It was decided that a dramatic statement should be made to the rebellious colonists. Something would be needed to demonstrate British strength and the futility of resistance.

One colonist, John Hancock of Boston, had past due accounts with the commissioners. The Earl thought to make an example of this young upstart.

On April 8, 1767, John Hancock's ship *Lydia* was seized by customs officials. It was the beginning of a long and costly battle with British authorities designed to bring him to his knees as an example to other colonists. It was a warning that public boldness would come at a terrible price. History shows convincingly that they picked the wrong man. Hancock eventually won the first round with British authorities. The seizure was later determined by England's own courts to be illegal, but the battle was costly and the commissioners were not through with Hancock.

Nearly a month later on the 4th of May, Hancock was reelected as one of Boston's representatives. He received an even higher honor when his peers elected him as a councilor. But the colonial governor would not have it. He erased John Hancock's name and demanded that they choose another.

On the evening of May 9, 1767, Hancock's ship *Liberty* arrived at Boston harbor. English customs officials decided that since the light was fading they would wait until morning to inspect the ship's cargo. However, the enterprising captain of Hancock's ship decided that there was plenty of light and ordered his crew to work through the night unloading the cargo, hoping to avoid being taxed. The next morning, customs officers arrived to find the captain lying dead on the deck. Doctors determined he had died from "overheating" (sic.). The ship was carrying only a small fraction of its capacity.

The incident exploded into public controversy with no one willing to speak out in defense of the "rich rebel" of Boston. Relentless British authorities eventually found a witness who testified that the captain had ordered the ship to be unloaded, and that much of the wine on board had been taken away during the night.

Apparently isolated and alone, the controversial John Hancock was now in serious trouble. Sir John Hallowell, the leading customs commissioner, ordered the ship seized and then decided to go to the scene himself to be sure that the job was done properly. But British authorities had underestimated the popularity of the rich Bostonian who constantly risked his fortune and his business to protest heavy-handed British colonial policy. Upon Hallowell's arrival, a crowd of hundreds of angry Bostonians had spontaneously gathered at the harbor. Hallowell and another official, Joseph Harrison, were chased to their homes, forced to dodge rocks the whole way. Both men were lucky to have lived through the ordeal.

Faced with overwhelming opposition, the ever expedient and patient British authorities backed down, seeking a compromise with John Hancock, the new hero of Boston. Hancock would be given back *Liberty* as long as he would make it available for the court's judgment. Both parties agreed this would be the best resolution. Once more the people of Boston cheered their courageous and cavalier merchant who had defied the British and seemingly prospered by doing so.

Inevitably, John Hancock's spreading fame began to trigger criticism. After the fact, Whig leaders tried to characterize Hancock's "deal" with customs officers as a compromise. The ever audacious and fearless Boston merchant countered by announcing that the deal was off. If any of his fellow colonists thought it a compromise, he would have none of it. The British could keep his ship. The incident only shamed his critics while deeply moving his supporters. They did not fail to notice that none of Hancock's critics were giving up ships and money and business to stand up to the oppressive British.

Afraid, and probably a little nervous about the recent uprisings, the Earl of Hillsborough demanded that Governor Bernard order the Massachusetts House to take back the Circular Letter. This letter, presented in February of 1768, spoke of the Massachusetts' House disgust of the unfair British government and taxation. He also ordered troops be sent from New York to Boston to be sure the people showed proper respect for the King.

When the demand was given to the Massachusetts House from Governor Bernard, John Hancock was enthusiastically selected to give the response. It was an earlier, colonial equivalent of General McAuliffe's famous response to the German army demanding surrender from the beleaguered American forces at Bastogne. During the World War II Battle of the Bulge, General McAuliffe responded to the Germans with one word—"Nuts."

In July of 1768, John Hancock was once again speaking about a new and improved nonimportation agreement among the Merchants Standing Committee. This time the merchants would declare a complete boycott of British goods. For one year, nothing except necessities would be allowed into the country. Tea, paper, glass, and painter's colors would be given a permanent boycott, rescinded only with the repeal of the despised Townsend Acts.

The Arrival of the Redcoats

Only thirty days after Hancock's announced boycott, the *Boston Weekly News Letter* published a little noticed report on the landing of British troops in Halifax, Nova Scotia. This news caused little comment from Bostonians until additional news reached them that the troops were headed their way. The commander confirmed that their final destination would be Boston.

The General Court set up a committee with Hancock as a member, demanding an explanation of the King's actions. The colonial governor feigned surprise, insisting to colonists that he knew nothing about the arriving force. In response, Hancock's committee held a statewide meeting for "all concerned citizens in Massachusetts." The turnout was huge, clearly indicating the entire colony's disgust with Governor Bernard and above all, Great Britain. The protest and numerous written inquiries from Boston citizens were ignored by the governor. Days later several thousand British troops marched into Boston, parading dramatically down the streets of the city in a show of force and finally turning the center of town into an armed camp. John Hancock looked helplessly out of his own second floor window at the camp fires burning on his lawn. Bostonians were desperate for a plan.

The sensational events unfolding in Boston very quickly became international news. *The New York Journal of Occurrences* distributed throughout the thirteen colonies and Britain, prominently featured the story, describing John Hancock as a local leader of the opposition and painting him as "the ultimate patriot."

Just before the end of the summer, British troops were put on alert. Arodi Thayer, Marshal of the Vice-Admiralty Court, was going to be making a call on the controversial Mr. John Hancock. It was not going to be a social call. There could be trouble. Thayer served Hancock with a warrant. It was the final settlement on the *Liberty* affair. British authorities, determined to break the "rich rebel," were demanding a fine of 9,000 pieces of silver sterling. It was an impossible demand designed to bring Hancock and all of his enterprises to their knees. Nevertheless, with the help of his lawyer and future president, John Adams, Hancock once more beat the odds. After a feeble attempt at prosecution, the charges were dropped.

Emboldened by his narrow escape, John Hancock shook himself off and went on the counterattack. He and the other representatives of Boston went to the governor demanding the evacuation of British troops from the city center. "They have turned the streets of Boston into one large latrine," they said. The governor refused and instead expelled the representatives from Boston, hoping a change of scenery would cool them off.

Once more an attempt at censure politically backfired. The representatives would not back down and their new pleas calling for the removal of Governor Bernard received wide and sympathetic coverage. When the King recalled his colonial governor for "consultations," the city of Boston broke into wild celebrations. Hancock and his friends marched back into the city. Governor Bernard would never return.

Betrayal

At the height of his popularity and acclaim, John Hancock faced his most bitter challenge. It didn't come from his British tormentors but rather from a fellow colonist, a loyalist, who some historians suggest had grown jealous and resentful of "the rich rebel."

John Mein, a Scottish immigrant, had opened a shop in Boston several years before the *Liberty* incident. In time he had prospered, and seeking to diversify his income, he had founded a newspaper, the *Boston Chronicle*. Within months the *Chronicle* became the *Gazette's* most successful competitor. Mein made no secret of his contempt for the so-called "patriots" and was quick to print pieces from London articles denouncing American patriotism as no more than "selfish greed."

Needless to say, such articles left the patriots fuming. In response, the *Gazette* published a letter by the popular pamphleteer, James Otis, taking John Mein to task and defending the motives of "the patriots." Mein was enraged. After being given informal assurances that the British authorities would look the other way, Mein decided to go after his antagonist. After a cursory investigation, a British informer mistakenly passed along the word that the offending article had been written by *Gazette* editor Johnathan Gill. One night, Mein ambushed Gill, assaulting him with a wooden club, leaving him on the street for dead. Gill survived and lived to testify against the publisher in court where John Mein was fined 130 sovereigns and released.

In the weeks that followed, Mein's newspaper began a steady drum beat of articles attacking the credibility and motives of "the patriots." John Hancock was portrayed as a hypocrite who continually violated his very own nonimportation boycott. At first, a dubious Boston public defended the integrity of their hero, but with time, the continual daily charges began to wear on Hancock's reputation. Risking life and fortune in his struggles with the British had been one thing, but risking one's reputation and the esteem of one's own peers was something altogether different.

In desperation, Hancock ordered his own investigation of Jonathan Mein, and in the process, gained critical information. It seemed that Hancock and Mein shared many of the same London suppliers including a Mr. Thomas Longman. While Hancock paid his bills promptly, Mein seemed to be accumulating a significant debt, much of which was owed to Longman. Hancock promptly petitioned the London supplier, offering to serve as his attorney in the collection of the debt. Within a few short months the cumbersome paperwork was completed. Hancock's most bitter enemy was cornered. Hancock now had the legal authority to enforce the repayment of Longman's debt.

This wearing, seesaw battle was now reaching a climax. Mein's *Boston Chronicle* unleashed another round of inflammatory charges against "the patriots," these more derogatory than any that had preceded them. John Hancock, James Otis, and the whole list of "patriots" were smeared. The public reacted immediately. Huge crowds protested outside the *Chronicle's* doors. Tension mounted. Loyalists, fearful for Mein's life, now urged him to flee the colonies. Perhaps thinking that he might also escape his enormous debt, Mein finally arranged passage to London. But John Hancock had anticipated this contingency, and he and Longman had already made arrangements for it. Upon arrival in London, Jonathan Mein was arrested on the docks and thrown into a London debtors prison.

Although he was gone, the loyalist publisher of the *Boston Chronicle* had left his mark. Bitterness between patriots and loyalists was acute. Violence was now commonplace. And yet miraculously, no one had died. That was to change.

The Boston Massacre

On the night of February 22, 1770, an angry patriot gang formed in Boston. They were targeting merchants who had ignored the nonimportation agreement. The gang protested briefly in the town center and then marched off toward the shop of loyalist Thomas Lille. A local customs official, Ebenezer Richardson, ordered the mob to halt and attempted to stop the crowd from destroying Lille's shop. Instead, the threatening mob grew more powerful, chasing the beleaguered customs official into Lille's house. When leaders among the mob began to force open the door, Richardson panicked and fired his pistol out the window. He later testified that he was only trying to frighten the mob away, but his bullet struck and killed a young German immigrant by the name of Christopher Seider. The following morning the *Boston Gazette* blared the story from its front pages. Seider was declared a martyr, a patriotic hero. The colonies were outraged. Boston was shocked and boiling with anger.

On March 5, 1770, an anti-British demonstration held in Boston grew to such numbers that the local colonial authorities called on British troops to restore order. When the redcoats arrived they were greeted with hoots of derision. Some young Bostonians began tossing snowballs into the lines of advancing soldiers. For a moment, that famous British soldierly discipline failed. Nervous redcoats spontaneously open fired. Officers ordered them to halt but dozens of unarmed colonists lay bleeding in the snow. Five died.

The next morning, John Hancock and his committee demanded an audience with Thomas Hutchinson, the acting governor of Massachusetts. "The troops would have to go," Hancock warned. Hutchinson and the British Colonel Dalrymple, agreed. The redcoats were marched out of the city. Boston had been liberated, for the moment.

Throughout the summer of 1770 a growing majority in Parliament began urging accommodation with the thirteen American colonies. In a sweeping move, Parliament repealed almost all of the provisions of the hated Townsend Act. Only the tax on tea would remain in effect and even that was kept as a symbolic face-saving gesture. Since the colonists had especially proclaimed to the world their bitter opposition to the tea tax, it would be kept as a statement to other colonies that Britannia still ruled over her far-flung empire.

With the growing moderation in England, many colonists urged restraint. Their agitation and anti-British demonstrations had made their point. Now negotiations were working. John Hancock fiercely argued in favor of maintaining the boycott to the end. Only when the tea tax was dropped should they give in, he maintained, but moderation was the order of the day. One by one, the little towns and villages of New England voted to drop their nonimportation pledges. Eventually, after resisting an impassioned plea from John Hancock, Boston merchants also ended the boycott.

The Boston Tea Party

In 1773, just when reasonable men on both sides of the Atlantic seemed to be in ascendance, Boston was racked by an enormous scandal. The Massachusetts House had long been responsible for setting the salary of its colonial governor. Feeling that their last governor, Bernard, had betrayed them, representatives had been cautiously optimistic about the work of his successor, Governor Hutchinson. Now the Court learned that for the past two years their own fellow American, Governor Hutchinson, had been on the King's personal payroll. Stunned by the news and what it might mean, Hancock and members of the House held a series of ad hoc meetings to discuss the ramifications. Most were bewildered and dispirited. Some merchants had lost their fortunes in the damaging politico-economic war with Britain. Now, who could they trust? Who else among them were agents of the Crown? How much damage had Hutchinson caused them in his dealings with London?

Even more shocking information was to follow. A package containing top secret letters was delivered to the Massachusetts House from Benjamin Franklin, the Pennsylvania colonial representative in London. The letters revealed that much of the chaos in Boston could be laid at the feet of two of their very own colonials, the aforementioned Governor Hutchinson and his brother-in-law, Andrew Oliver. Among other things, the letters showed the treacherous and duplicitous role the governor had played. When British troops had landed, he had feigned surprise and spent many long hours discussing with colonial representatives on the proper reaction. Now the letters revealed that he himself had secretly urged the King to dispatch the Royal Expeditionary Force. The redcoats had marched into Boston at his invitation and he was responsible for all of the terror that had followed.

John Hancock made sure that the notorious letters were published. The colonies were in an uproar. The Massachusetts House demanded the governor's discharge. Day by day, the scandal grew. Members of the House learned that Hutchinson had been working with the King to affect a monopoly on the tea business. The Crown had chosen five close, political allies as their exclusive "tea agents" in America. Number one and number two on the list were Thomas Hutchinson and his brother, Elisha.

A boisterous town meeting was held in Boston to discuss the latest news of the spreading scandal. In the meantime, John Hancock was dispatched to the governor to demand the immediate relinquishment of the monopoly. But the governor, whose country home was now extensively fortified and guarded by armed troops, rejected the demands out of hand.

On November 28, 1773, the House received word that the ship *Dartmouth*, had arrived at Boston harbor. Its cargo holds were full of tea. Debate raged back and forth between representatives on what action could be taken. Within a few days, the *Dartmouth* was joined by the *Eleanor* and the *Beaver*, both ships also carrying tea. On December 16, one thousand patriots dressed like Indians, their faces smeared with war paint, swarmed out of the Old South Meeting House and descended on Boston Harbor. While their war whoops and some laughter echoed across the water, the patriots dumped the tea into the sea.

The famous Boston Tea Party stirred the colonies and ignited the imagination of the world. Even the moderate Bostonian, John Adams, was moved by the bold action.

"The British will not take this lightly," he warned friends, "There is no turning back now."

In the days following these dramatic events, John Hancock's health took a turn for the worse. He was bedridden. Rumors spread around the city that he had given up. Perhaps he was joining with the loyalists in their tea monopoly. However, on the anniversary of the Boston Massacre in 1774, Hancock dragged himself out of bed to give the most powerful, patriotic speech of his life. The crowd was awestruck by his words which condemned the loyalists and "their redcoats" stationed around the city. His moving account, retelling the events of that horrible night, left all who listened in tears.

John Hancock's speech reestablished his place in Massachusetts politics, but he was unable to enjoy his new found celebrity. Once more he was forced to return to his bedroom to recover from his illness. It was during this convalescence that his worried Aunt Lydia invited a young woman named Dorothy "Dolly" Quincy to stay with them and help care for her nephew. Dolly soon proved to be more than a cure for the "rich rebel." From the very first day a romance was born.

The Intolerable Acts

In the immediate months following the Boston Tea Party, the King of England and the British Parliament came down on the colonies with an iron hand. If such rebellion became contagious and spread to other colonies it would mean the end of British rule. There must be a price for such resistance and it must be high. At the King's insistence Parliament passed a series of laws which became known as the Intolerable Acts. They were as follows:

1. The Boston Port Act essentially shut down the entire city. It closed the harbor, preventing any cargo from coming in or going out. This alone would bring Boston's merchants to their knees.

2. The Massachusetts Bay Government Act gave the governor exclusive power over every political occurrence in his state. Rights were taken away from the representatives, giving only the governor power to elect council members and county sheriffs. Most obnoxious of all, town meetings would henceforth be illegal except for one annual meeting where discussion would consist only of elections and ordinances.

3. The Administration of Justice Act gave the governor power to send officials charged with committing a crime directly to England for trial and punishment. The citizens of Boston knew that this meant privileged treatment for all Crown officials, allowing them to get away with any crime, including murder. Henceforth, it was nicknamed the "Murderer's Act."

4. The Quartering Act allowed the British troops to invade Boston again, giving them power to take over any unoccupied building they saw fit.

Momentarily stunned and frightened, Boston merchants met to discuss their options. John Hancock courageously led the charge. They should not only stop importation altogether, he exclaimed, but exportation as well. If the harbor was shut down, the merchants should not trade for any English goods whatsoever. If it meant bankruptcy, so be it. Let the English suffer too.

Meanwhile, the appointment of the new Massachusetts governor was a political masterstroke. Ironically, General Thomas Gage, commander of the Royal Expeditionary Force in America, was well-known and widely respected in Boston. While he served the King, he was a good listener who had shown an uncanny ability to understand the American side of an issue, or at least, so the moderate colonists believed. The British knew that with Gage in control, the redcoats would be able to march back into Boston without incident. Crowds on the streets of Boston greeted Gage with smiles, but it was not to last. The House very quickly realized that Gage was not going to be their ally. The commander vetoed all but five of the eighteen nominations for the Council. Then, he ordered the representatives to meet in Salem, not Boston.

Within months the full power of the Intolerable Acts hit the city of Boston with all its fury. Unemployment shot up. Bread lines formed and beggars filled the streets.

Crime surged. Violence erupted between citizens and soldiers.

Meanwhile, John Hancock began calling for an intercolonial congress to meet and discuss the growing conflict with the Crown. There was a precedent for such an idea. The colonies had sent delegates to a joint meeting in Albany the year before. In 1774, a Continental Congress convened in Philadelphia. Five representatives were sent from Boston; James Bowdoin, Thomas Cushing, Samuel Adams, John Adams, and Robert Treat Paine. John Hancock, the man who had first called for the meeting, was asked to stay behind to handle the tenuous crisis in Boston.

The problems in the Massachusetts colony were growing daily and so were the protests. A worried Governor Gage called for a meeting of the Massachusetts House in Salem on October 5, 1774. Then, deciding that he could accomplish nothing with its angry members, refused to show up for his own meeting. Infuriated by the snub, angry representatives took the governing of Massachusetts into their own hands. They set up a congress, chose John Hancock as their president and formed an emergency militia dubbed the "Minute Men." The new Massachusetts militia must be ready for a call to arms with only a minute's notice.

Meanwhile, the Continental Congress in Philadelphia declared the Port Act void. Henceforth, Boston Harbor would be open for importing and exporting. Also, the Congress determined it was right to expect and prepare for an attack from Great Britain. When James Bowdoin became ill, the Congress called John Hancock to Philadelphia as his replacement.

The "rich rebel's" growing power in the colonies put his life in great danger. During the annual Massacre Day oration, a large number of heavily armed British soldiers appeared, blocking the entrances and aisles of the hall. It was rumored that if the speaker, a Mr. Joseph Warren, were to say anything negative about the King, a soldier was to throw an egg at him signaling the others to begin fighting. In the melee, selected assassins were to kill John Hancock and Samuel Adams. Such stories gained credence when colonists made public the secret accounts of British involvement in the assassination of Indian Chief Pontiac several years before. Friends warned Hancock to stay in Philadelphia, if not to protect himself, at least for the sake of his Aunt Lydia and his fiancée Dolly, whose lives were also in danger.

The War of Independence

Governor Thomas Gage, the man that many colonists had once looked to as a moderating influence between loyalists and patriots, now became the trigger of war. Gage, a military commander who was used to issuing orders and seeing them carried out, had grown tired of watching the rebellion spread across his colony. It was time to strike back at the defiance. Gage ordered his soldiers to Concord to arrest the highly visible John Hancock and Samuel Adams.

Thus began the American Revolution. Paul Revere, a Boston dentist and engraver, began his famous ride to Concord, shouting, "The British are coming!" He was joined by another rider, William Dawes, and then another, Dr. Samuel Prescott. All three were stopped and captured by the loyalist armies. Revere was arrested. Dawes was forced to turn back. But Prescott escaped and forged ahead to warn Concord.

Fearing for his life and convinced by friends that he was worth more to the revolution alive than dead, Samuel Adams fled Concord. The ever-courageous Hancock refused all such arguments. He would stay, he vowed, joining the patriot armies in their preparation for battle. By the following morning, patriot military leaders had decided that this was a battle they couldn't win. That evening, under cover of darkness, they abandoned Concord. Hancock carefully made arrangements for Lydia and Dolly to live with Thaddeus Burr in Fairfield, Connecticut. He then escaped without a moment to spare. For the next few years he would live his life on the run.

The following year, with the war now raging in pitched battles all across Massachusetts, the two most famous American fugitives, John Hancock and Samuel Adams, were reunited in Philadelphia at the Second Continental Congress. John was not the only new member; there were two others, Benjamin Franklin and Thomas Jefferson. On the first ballot, John Hancock was unanimously elected president of the Congress.

While the politicians were seeking answers in Philadelphia, each local colony was busy recruiting militiamen to help defend itself. In June, Massachusetts patriots intercepted plans for the redcoats to seize the heights overlooking the Boston center. When British troops arrived at the hills, the patriots were waiting. The fierce battle of Bunker Hill, fought by the Continental Congress's newly adopted army, formerly known as John Hancock's Massachusetts Minutemen, was an eye opener both to the colonists and their English masters. Eventually, British troops took the heights, but in the process they lost nearly 1,000 soldiers, three times the American casualties.

It was a sobering lesson for the British. The American frontiersmen, even without formal military training, were not going to be pushovers. And the patriots, so sure that they could hold the heights forever had lost them in a few hours, feeling for the first time the power of British gunboats firing off the coast and British cannons decimating their ranks from a distance. There was a reason that the British had been able to build an empire. The American War for Independence was not going to be easy for either side.

The Declaration of Independence

With the dramatic news from Boston, John Hancock received a startling personal message from his Aunt Lydia. She wanted him to know that a Mr. Aaron Burr, the nephew of their host, Thaddeus Burr, was making visits to the house in Fairfield. It was a clear warning. If John still held any attachment for Dolly, he had better hustle back to take care of things. Hancock could not stand the thought of Aaron Burr courting "his Dolly." The next day he rode to Fairfield and proposed. On August 28, 1775, John Hancock and Dorothy Quincy became man and wife.

In spite of war, the future looked bright for John Hancock. It was true that he was still the most wanted man in America, with British authorities offering a bounty for his head. But he had finally married Dolly and enjoyed a prestigious position as president of the Continental Congress. They lived in relative safety in Philadelphia, miles from the turmoil in Massachusetts. The following year, there was the happy news that she was pregnant. It was also true that Hancock's work as a politician had left him little time for business. The crisis in Boston had resulted in a long list of debtors unable to ever repay him. Even when the city was eventually relieved, he found his warehouses and office buildings totally destroyed. He had built it all once before, and together with Dolly and Lydia, he would build it again.

Then came the news of his Aunt Lydia's sudden death. John and Dolly found themselves unable to cope. She had been like a mother to both of them. Dolly was especially affected. She worried over their precarious financial situation. She worried about their personal safety. How could she live alone with a baby if an assassin's bullet should take her husband?

On July 4, 1776, the Second Continental Congress finally accepted Thomas Jefferson's written Declaration of Independence. In defiance of Great Britain, the thirteen

American colonies were declaring their freedom. As president of the Congress, John Hancock was the first to sign. Many others would sign in the months following, with the last signature received on November 4. Hancock courageously endorsed the document in large, bold print, saying, "There! John Bull can read my name without his spectacles and may now double the reward on my head. That is my defiance."

For John and Dolly Hancock, the Revolutionary War years brought with them a mixed blessing of public success and personal tragedy. The threat of invasion forced the Congress to flee to Baltimore, and then back again to Philadelphia, and thence to Lancaster and eventually York, Pennsylvania. Boston was alternately liberated and occupied again. The Hancock home was robbed. Their new baby girl was born, and was named Lydia. But shortly after her first birthday, she became ill and died. The uncertainty and dangers of war forced long months of depressing separation.

After giving much of his adult life to public service, John Hancock finally resigned from the Continental Congress to return to private life and his beloved Dolly. After a two-year absence, he rode into Boston a national hero and a figure of international fame, whose name was synonymous with personal courage and boldness.

Reunited, John and Dolly determined to recreate the pleasant memories of an earlier time in Boston. With the war swirling around them, they entertained visiting French military advisors, and listened sympathetically to the concerns of the common people. He patiently accepted the thanks of soldiers who sometimes waited in lines outside their home to catch a glimpse of the hero of the revolution. Once more, the Hancock home became the center of life in Boston. On May 21, 1778, John George Washington Hancock was born. They were a family again.

When the new Massachusetts Constitution created a position of governor, John Hancock was elected in a landslide victory. Reinvigorated by public acclaim, the "rich rebel" devoted all of his energies and all of the Massachusetts state resources to winning the war. Eventually, with the help of the French, the Continental armies were able to drive the British out of nearly every occupied town in the state. The redcoats knew there was little hope and finally surrendered to the armies of George Washington on October 21, 1781. America's longest war was over.

A Fortune Lost

John Hancock's life had never been easy. From the early death of his father, to the loss of his uncle, to a life on the run with a price on his head, Hancock had always bravely and resiliently bounced back. When the whole wealth and power of the British Crown focused angrily and exclusively on him, attempting to destroy his business and even take his life, he had boldly and courageously fought back and won. It was a life that typified the brave and independent spirit of a new, emerging race of people.

And yet, when he reached his fifties, the toll of such battles began to reflect itself in his deteriorating health.

John and Dolly were to receive one last blow. In January 1787 their healthy and vibrant young son left the house with his ice skates over his shoulder. Moments later he fell and struck his head. He died a short while later. The Hancocks had lost their only surviving child.

In 1788, when the newly organized United States of America held its first national election, there was never any doubt that George Washington, Commander of the Revolutionary Forces, would be elected president. But under the new constitution, the vice president would be the runner-up in the presidential voting. Enthusiastic citizens of Massachusetts promoted their longtime governor, John Hancock, the man who had boldly signed his name in large script to the Declaration of Independence. For several months, Hancock's name led all speculation for the position, but the fact was that the governor was seriously ill and eventually much of the country knew it. John Adams, "the moderate," and cousin to Hancock's old revolutionary partner Samuel Adams, was elected to the post and went on to become the second U. S. president.

When the announcement came that the new president and American hero, George Washington, would be visiting Boston, the city came alive with excitement and special preparation. The city planned a huge welcoming party and a reunion of Revolutionary War heroes. Of course, Governor John Hancock desperately wanted to go and preside over the great events. It would be a crowning celebration of a lifetime of dreams and hopes for his beloved Boston. However, John Hancock was dying. Doctors ordered him to stay in his bed.

On that great day, as events unfolded, a steady stream of couriers brought news by the hour. When by midday, the governor learned that the new president had been insulted by his absence, John Hancock overruled his doctors and ordered his bed be carried to the celebration. As in all the misunderstandings and crises he had faced before, Hancock knew that direct confrontation was the best. It has been said that when George Washington saw the emaciated body of John Hancock on that day, he wept at the sight of him and apologized profusely.

On September 18, 1793, fifty-seven-year-old Governor John Hancock appeared at the front of the Massachusetts Assembly for the last time. On October 8, he arose from his sleep like any other day. A few minutes later, he found it nearly impossible to breathe. He was dead within the hour.

At thirty-one years of age, John Hancock had single-handedly financed the Boston rebellion. As the city's wealthiest merchant, he had completely underwritten the Sons of Liberty, paid for drink and food for patriots at the Liberty Tree tavern, and financed banners and pamphlets promoting the cause of independence. In spite of his great wealth and the fact that he had more than anyone else to lose, John Hancock had initiated and organized the nonimportation boycott of British goods. At thirty-five he organized the Minutemen, the first American army, paying for their green uniforms and buying their ammunition. At thirty-nine, he presided over the Second Continental

Congress, picking up the tab for housing and food for some of the poorer members.

Yet when he died, there was virtually nothing left. John Hancock, the "rich rebel," died penniless. The man whose name is forever associated with personal bravery and boldness had given everything he had for freedom.

"...and for the support of this declaration...we mutually pledge to each other our lives, our fortunes, and our sacred honor." Hancock, who signed first, gave them all.

COURAGE

"If I were asked to give what I consider the single most useful bit of advice it would be this: Expect trouble as an inevitable part of life and when it comes, hold your head high, look it squarely in the eye and say 'I will be bigger than you. You can not defeat me.'"
– Ann Landers

This most admired of the leadership qualities is often the most misunderstood. We revel in the accomplishments of our war heroes because of their willingness to stand their ground and face their attackers. We love to see ourselves in their place. When speaking to some of our decorated heroes, you will find that they admit to being just as afraid as any of their fellow soldiers, some even more so. The thing that made them different was their reaction to fear. They chose, at that particular moment, to attack the thing that made them most afraid, instead of running from it.

We invoked the story of John Hancock to illustrate the brash boldness of the American personality. In truth, all of the early revolutionary personalities were heroic figures of their time. As author of the Declaration of Independence, Thomas Jefferson would have been the first to hang. His name aroused even more anger than the courageous John Hancock, who boldly and provocatively signed the document in large script. George Washington was a constant target of assassination. During a three year period, John Paul Jones risked life and limb almost daily on his own initiative, taking the battle for liberty to the shores of the enemy.

> *"This country was not built by men who relied on somebody else to take care of them. It was built by men who relied on themselves, who dared to shape their own lives, who had enough courage to blaze new trails — enough confidence in themselves to take the necessary risks."*
> *– Robert J. McCracken*

To be successful in any enterprise one must be willing to act; to buy, sell, borrow, loan, to speak up, or to move. Action means life, resignation means death. Often, it is the lack of action that causes one to fail. Ironically, many people are afraid of failing so they bring about their own destruction by simply choosing not to act. Do not be afraid of attempting something great in your life because you may fail; without the attempt, failure is certain.

When discussing this principle with those that have displayed it, they will tell you that it was a result of preparation, of practice. When the time came, their reactions were second nature because of the countless hours, weeks, or years spent rehearsing.

One of the easiest ways to find courage, once you have trained yourself in whatever you are pursuing, is simply not to look for it. Courage finds you when you need it most. So, if you are afraid, then you are like anyone else that has displayed the principle of courage. Embrace this similarity, because it will give you the ability to accomplish great things.

"No sane man is unafraid in battle, but discipline produces in him a form of vicarious courage."
– General George S. Patton, Jr.

Chapter Four

John Paul Jones - Perseverance At Any Cost

"I have not yet begun to fight."
– John Paul Jones

If vision and courage were already in the hearts of American immigrants even before hitting the shores, the American penchant for "winning," for persevering, for never giving up, was a quality that developed on this side of the Atlantic.

Consider that almost 300 years elapsed between Columbus' voyage and the birth of the United States. It has been just over 200 years since. The American personality was almost three centuries in the making. Perseverance was born out of necessity. The Pilgrims had to learn how to farm or die. They had to learn how to defend themselves from the Indians and wild beasts of the forests or die. They had to learn how to survive the winters or die. In fact, the first settlements did perish.

It was survival, not money, not fame, not self-esteem that motivated the first Americans. But it is safe to say that in the process of surviving, Americans discovered the power of stubborn persistence. What was born out of necessity eventually became an acquired characteristic. They learned the secret of victory: stubborn commitment. They developed the habit of winning. By the 1770s, Patrick Henry proclaimed, "Give me liberty or give me death!"

What had once been necessary for survival would now help them get what they wanted: independence from Great Britain. Americans would win, not because they were the strongest or smartest, but because they were the most stubborn. They would never give up.

> *"We fight, get beat, rise, and fight again."*
> *– Major General Nathaniel Greene*

John Paul Jones, America's greatest naval hero, grandly typifies the stubbornness and persistence that is part of the American formula for success. From steel magnate Andrew Carnegie to football coach Vince Lombardi, Americans have made a creed out of winning. In business, in sports, in war, giving up is out of the question. Speaking to a university graduating class, President Calvin Coolidge said that perseverance was more important than any other "virtue" and the key to "all successful accomplishments."

A Humble Beginning

Jones was actually born John Paul; that is, Paul was his last name. The addition of "Jones" would come later, when in desperate times he was forced to seek a new identity. John Paul was born on July 6, 1747, in Kirkbean, Scotland. His parents were servants to a wealthy landowner. His father, John Paul, Sr., worked as a gardener, while mother, Jean, was the housekeeper. The family lived in a cottage just outside the manor. Although the Pauls were not wealthy and came from a humble social station, they were well taken care of by their employer who trusted them and greatly depended on them.

John attended school at the local Presbyterian church headed by the Reverend James Hogg. The young Mr. Paul was a good student, but no match for some of his classmates whose work under the expert tutelage of Reverend Hogg won them scholarships to study in Edinburgh and London. With many of his friends now at the university and his father urging him to pursue a worthy vocation, John Paul, Jr. took to the sea. From earliest memories, the ocean had held a special fascination for the youth. When his older brother, William, immigrated to the American colonies, John Paul carefully staked out the journey on maps, imagining himself on such an adventure. When a close friend had once pressed him about his future, he admitted that he had no idea where fate was taking him, but somehow, in some way, he would make sure that it would be "to the high seas." He was only thirteen when he became an apprentice on the fishing vessel, *Friendship,* which was bound for America. So began the adventure.

The American Experience

John Paul was immediately taken by life in the American colonies. His older brother, William, was now a well-known tailor in the bustling and important port city of Fredricksburg, Virginia. Some of the most important men in the city stopped by the shop to be fitted by William Paul. The Reverend Patrick Henry, uncle to the famous orator, was a rector of a nearby church. In one of the taverns of Fredricksburg, a famous young veteran of the French and Indian Wars, by the name of George Washington, came often to play cards and to discuss the despised Stamp Acts. Wagon trains laden with grain and in lines stretching for miles, frequently creaked down from the mountains and up the cobblestone streets to the Fredricksburg wharf. Captains and sailors moved constantly through the town.

William introduced John Paul to the emerging Virginia aristocracy. This was a splendid, unique society, where knowledge and reason and one's conduct as a gentleman were more important than the social station of one's parents. John Paul jumped into the discussions with boyish enthusiasm and was soon reading and writing and studying the great works of his day.

Still, the lure of the sea continually seduced him. He made several more voyages between England, America, and the West Indies, gaining more experience and ability. By the time he reached nineteen, he had become the first mate on the slaver, *Two Friends*.

Repulsed by the barbaric slave trade, John Paul would not stay with the ship for long. In 1768, at the age of twenty-one, he found himself stranded and unemployed in the West Indies. Never the kind to relish inactivity, on a whim, he boldly auditioned for a part in the theater company of John Moody, the famous Irish actor. A surprised John Paul won the role of young "Bevil" in *The Conscious Lovers*, and toured Jamaica with the famous actor. Though the tour was brief, the experience left an indelible mark. He left the stage with a new appreciation for the sense of the dramatic, the commanding use of his voice and bodily gestures, and the impact it could all have on other people. Young John Paul now had a charisma or "presence," as his contemporaries called it, that would mark his character for life.

The following year John Paul returned to his true love— the ocean. He announced to friends that he was now committed to a maritime career. This time his perseverance paid off. Trade between the Caribbean and the Continent was booming and the young Mr. Paul's career was in full ascendancy. Within a few months he was given command of his first ship. The enterprising Scottish sailor, in spite of a quick temper, was fast developing a distinguished career as a merchant captain. Then, an incident took place in the summer of 1770 which would haunt him to the end of his life.

Captain Paul's ship lay at anchor in Rockley Bay in the West Indian island of Tobago. For days it sat in the harbor while the ship's young carpenter, Mungo Maxwell, tried to make late repairs. Only weeks before, Maxwell had neglected his duties, arrogantly ignoring the captain's warnings. There was an escalating tension between the two, exacerbated by the tremendous financial cost of the delays. When Maxwell openly disobeyed the captain's order, John Paul's temper flared. On a ship, the captain's word was law. He grabbed a whip and lashed it across the carpenter's shoulders again and again, raising bruised welts.

113

Captain Paul was charged with assault in the Tobago courts, but the local magistrate ruled the incident as "acceptable punishment." At first, it appeared that the Maxwell affair would pass. The carpenter left for another ship and John Paul's crew publicly ignored the incident and went back to work. Only a few weeks later, however, Mungo Maxwell died at sea. According to his captain, he had succumbed to a "fever and lowness of spirits." When John Paul returned to Scotland, he was greeted with the news that he would be tried for Maxwell's death.

Captain John Paul was eventually acquitted of all charges and fully exonerated by the British court. But in 1773, a new, more serious charge was leveled at the young captain. Once more, while laying anchor in Tobago, John Paul lashed out at an unruly crew member. John had promised to pay his crew upon arrival at the Caribbean island, but a change in fortunes dictated otherwise. Now, Paul announced he was withholding the pay until their return to Great Britain. They needed enough money for a full return cargo. He would still guarantee their salaries, he assured them, but they would have to wait.

This announcement was met with bitter opposition from a crew that had been counting the days until they could take leave on the Caribbean island. There was a mutiny and the ring leader was killed by John's own hand. That evening, the captain was given the news that he would likely be charged with murder. A friend of the court warned that he would not get off so lightly this time. John Paul was told that he should now abandon any hope of a naval career. The authorities would be looking for him at every port. John Paul fled into the night. Several years later, a young seaman by the name of John Paul "Jones" surfaced in America. He was a homely, thin, young man, five feet six inches tall, and well-built, much as the murderer in Tobago. The only difference was his name.

A Revolutionary Career

Times were uncertain in the American colonies. The Boston Tea Party, the Intolerable Acts, and the nonimportation boycott of "the patriots" all contributed to the turmoil. At the outbreak of the Revolution, most merchants were grounded and Jones was unemployed. However, when the Continental Congress established a navy, John Paul Jones, through the influence of two friends, was commissioned a lieutenant.

On December 3, 1775, on board the *Alfred*, he became the first American commander to hoist the Grand Union flag, a symbol of the colonies' disgust with the British. So began a short but sensational naval career that would astound his peers and enliven the history books.

First came his celebrated encounter with the British ship, *Glasgow*. Jones and his crew fought fiercely and bravely. Within days of the battle, he was promoted to Captain of the sloop, *Providence*.

The following month, Jones received a flattering letter written by John Hancock, Robert Morris, and Arthur Middleton, to name a few. These leading American merchants were so impressed with Jones' apparent audacity and fearlessness, that they successfully lobbied the U.S.

navy to have Jones and his crew separated from the rest of the American fleet and sent on an independent raid to the Bahamas. Knowing that any interruption of British trade would raise an uproar among investors in London, and thus perhaps speed an end to the war, Jones was instructed to seek and destroy or "make a prize" of any British ship.

It was a dashing assignment and Jones would succeed far beyond anyone's expectations. He had been sailing the Caribbean for years and knew every cove and isolated island. Before his orders could be changed, he set out immediately to sea. For forty-nine days, John Paul Jones sunk one ship after another, taking the bounty from dozens of others. One observer credited his victories, not to cunning or better strategies, but to the fact that he simply would not give up. Rather than outfight, he *outlasted* his opponents. He and his crew single-handedly wiped out the British fishing industry in the Bahamas. In the United States, where the people were hungry for news of any victory no matter how costly, Jones became a sensation. A hero was born. Stories of his dramatic exploits, his perseverance in battle, and his many narrow victories, spread through the colonies.

When the Marine Committee ordered four ships north for a campaign on the high seas off the Canadian coast, Jones was quickly recalled from his Caribbean campaign and given command of the *Alfred*. Once again, the Scotsman proved his skill. In a matter of days, he had captured five British ships all laden with valuable goods. One of his ships was immediately sent to North Carolina and put into action. Another he kept in his own squadron.

With the successful raid behind him, Jones headed to

Boston, the nearest port. Intercepting his small fleet enroute was a large warship. The sun was setting and the approaching vessel was in the shadows. Alarm bells started going off in Jones' head. His instincts were telling him that this was not a friendly ship. He was right. It was the powerful British man-o-war, *H.M.S. Milford*. As the ships sailed around a bend, the setting sun now burst upon the *Milford*, temporarily blinding the crew. John Paul Jones sent a series of deceptive signals, but he did not hesitate or veer from his course. Captain Burr of the *Milford* carefully read the messages and wrongly concluded that Jones's fleet was actually a group of merchantmen, escorted by the *H.M.S. Flora*. The powerful British warship reluctantly let them pass.

Early the next morning, Captain Burr realized his mistake and pursuit began. Burr recaptured one of the ships, but America's new war hero escaped him. John Paul Jones sailed into Boston harbor with the rest of his prizes intact. The embattled, blockaded city was ecstatic with joy. The taverns were filled with men retelling the story of how the British had been outfoxed. Within weeks, the U. S. Congress announced that it would be rewarding the brave, persistent, young captain by giving him command of a new, twenty-gun sloop.

The French Years

On June 14, 1777, the same day that Congress presented to the world the Stars and Stripes, the new flag of the United

States, John Paul Jones was presented with his new ship, *Ranger*, and ordered to sail for neutral harbors in France. He was to capture any enemy ships enroute.

Based in France, Jones made numerous surprise attacks on British vessels, capturing several ships his first few weeks. But with time, a daring idea began to form in his mind. He would attack the British when and where they would least expect it. He would raid the British Isles themselves.

In an ironic "homecoming," John Paul Jones and *Ranger* unexpectedly sailed out of the Irish Sea into Whitehaven, Scotland. As astonished villagers looked on, Jones and his crew set fire to the entire port, causing tremendous loss to the British. It was a stunning victory. The British not only lost all of the ships in the harbor, and mountains of supplies and stock in the warehouses on shore, it was a devastating blow to British pride and confidence.

Jones's daring raid had now aroused the fury of the world's most powerful navy. Ships sped to the area in an attempt to trap the American once and for all. A wise course would have been to find a safe harbor and lay low for awhile. Instead, Jones conceived of yet another exploit. He would sail into St. Mary's Isle in Scotland, kidnap the Earl of Selkirk, and demand the freedom of American prisoners as ransom.

At great risk, Jones managed to evade his British pursuers and sail undetected to St. Mary's Isle. After laying anchor, Jones and a raiding party descended on the Earl's manor only to find that he was not home. The gallant navy commander ordered his men not to touch Lady Selkirk or any of her servants. The Lady gracefully handed over some china and other belongings and then offered each member of the raiding party a glass of wine, plying them with questions about America. Captain Jones was very much taken with Lady Selkirk, later offering to return what was taken. But the gracious Lady would not accept. After all, it had all been won fairly in war and there was no greater honor than to be the victim of the famous American privateer, the man who never gave up, the stubborn Captain Jones.

Sailing out of the harbor of St. Mary's Isle, the American raider encountered the powerful and proud *H.M.S. Drake*. The captain of the *Drake* saw the famous *U.S.S. Ranger* and quickly raised the Union Jack. Jones raised the Stars and Stripes, a stunning sight for those waters. The battle was on. Once again, the American was victorious. Jones took the *Drake* as his prize, and all 200 crewmen became his prisoners. By the time the *U.S.S. Ranger* returned to French harbors, the American naval commander was world famous. The British were being embarrassed at their own game.

In the battle with the *Drake*, the *Ranger* had taken quite a beating. Jones immediately began searching for another ship. In February 1779, the War Department gave him command of the East India ship, *Duras*. Jones promptly renamed the vessel *Bonhomme Richard,* the French title for Benjamin Franklin's famous *Poor Richard's Almanac*. John Paul Jones, a fan of the wry sage Franklin, often quoted from the *Almanac* those famous lines, "If you would have your business done, go yourself; if not, send."

On August 14, 1779, Jones set out with a Franco-American squadron of seven ships (soon reduced to four), to do some more of his notorious raiding of the British. This time he sailed around the west coast of Ireland, and around his own native Scotland to the east Yorkshire coast, descending unexpectedly from the north. So unlikely was his route that more than seventeen ships were captured in the voyage and many more sent to the bottom of the sea. His warrior reputation was now at its height. Stories of his alleged terror spread among the British populous, who now clamored for his head. Not everyone was a fan, however. Jones had constant difficulties with Peter Landais, the French captain of the *Alliance,* one of the four ships in his squadron.

Into the History Books

On September 23, 1779, off Flamborough Head, the famous three-hour engagement with the *H.M.S. Serapis* ensued. Those bloody hours would rank as among the most desperate in American naval history.

The *H.M.S. Serapis*, commanded by Richard Pearson, was a new and gigantic frigate, which should easily have bested the *Bonhomme Richard.* Unfortunately for Captain Pearson, he was facing a man of great battle experience with dozens of such encounters already under his belt: a man of incalculable stubbornness and self confidence. Jones invoked all of his theatrical ability to inspire his crew.

They were told not to be intimidated by the size of the approaching *Serapis*. Instead, imagine the glory of conquering such a great ship, especially off the coast of Britain.

At first, Pearson was somewhat shocked that Jones and his *Bonhomme Richard* were not running away, but soon the power of the *Serapis* began to show. The two ships pounded each other, cannons blazing. It was a fierce menage of fire, smoke, and blood. Wounded men, some with their arms and legs blown off, were screaming out in pain and panic. The *Bonhomme* was severely damaged. It was at this point in the battle that Captain Pearson shouted a sarcastic remark across the water to the famous "pirate." The exact words of his taunt (probably something to the effect of "Have you had enough yet?") have been lost, but history has forever etched deeply in its pages the answer. Shouting above the din of battle, John Paul Jones announced, "I have not yet begun to fight!"

The two ships continued to blast one another, yard arm to yard arm, until the ships were hopelessly entangled. It was a lethal connection. The guns slammed against each other and many men died on both ships.

At the peak of the battle the remaining ships of the American and French squadron appeared. The crew of the *Bonhomme* cheered, but the drama was only reaching a more complex and treacherous phase. The willful Captain Landais of the *Alliance*, whom Jones previously had trouble with, saw the *Bonhomme* listing dangerously. Yet, she had done enough damage to the *Serapis* that it too was vulnerable. In a split second, the French commander apparently decided to sink them both. The famous Jones would be gone and a new naval hero, Landais, would be declared in his place, the surviving victor in this desperate battle with *Serapis*.

The French ship *Alliance* broadsided *Bonhomme* and *Serapis* indiscriminately, causing the *Bonhomme Richard* to begin sinking. If Jones did not know it before, he certainly knew now, that he was outnumbered and betrayed. His ship foundering, Jones quickly gave his men the signal for an old trick; he would attempt to lure the enemy onboard. With his men feigning defeat, some even diving overboard, the crew of the *Serapis* clamored over the sides to finish them off. Hand-to-hand combat broke out across the deck of the listing *Bonhomme*, with the men of the *Serapis* calling out, "We've got them!" When Pearson and his crew had fully committed themselves, Jones gave the order, and sailors who had been hiding under cover now poured out onto the deck to fight. The crew of the *Serapis* suddenly found itself outnumbered, its command divided.

With nearly all of his men killed, captured or wounded, Captain Pearson of the *Serapis* decided that surrender was the only option. Jones sent his lieutenant to bring Pearson onboard the *Bonhomme*. The British commander offered his sword to the victorious Jones, but the American commander refused it, offering instead his compliments to Pearson on a great fight. For a few minutes, the two men sat calmly in the captain's quarters of the *Bonhomme*, sharing a drink, as the famous ship burned and slowly sank.

On the deck of the American ship lay 67 dead and 106 wounded. Only 167 survived to tell the story to their grandchildren. On the smoldering deck of the *Serapis*, lay 100 dead and 121 wounded.

It was nearly midnight when the melancholy spectators onshore went home. It was not so easy onboard. The two rival surgeons, Dr. Brooke and Dr. Bannatyne, worked furiously hacking and bandaging. Carpenters also worked throughout the night, primarily on the American vessel. But the harder the craftsmen worked, the lower the *Richard* sank. At nine the next morning, her proud head dipped into the water. Jones abandoned her. Later he would write, "A little after ten I saw with inexpressible grief the last glimpse of the *Bonhomme Richard*."

Political worlds on both sides of the ocean were astounded by the action. The captain of a superior British warship had been captured by an inferior American craft — on the British ship's own coast!

This victory was to be Jones's crowning moment, the ultimate example of perseverance, and, as is often the case, the beginning of many great disappointments as well. He was now the relentless target of the entire British navy. Jones was then captured by the Dutch, who though neutral, insisted that Jones was only a pirate. When American diplomatic pressure secured his release, he preferred charges against the French Captain Landais and was able to take control of his ship, the *Alliance*.

As the war neared an end, Jones headquartered in France. Fate had cast him in the grand part of a dashing American Revolutionary War hero. Everywhere, especially in France, he was the subject of adulation and applause.

A Hero Returns

Detained longer than originally planned, Jones finally returned to America in February of 1781. He had been absent for over three years, but he was returning a hero. A week after his arrival, the American Congress honored him with the momentous Cross of the Institution of Military Merit for his "high sense of distinguished bravery and military conduct." Later, Jones would receive the Gold Medal "in commendation of his valor and brilliant services," the only officer of the Continental navy thus distinguished.

Some of the older officers remonstrated against the ensuing honors awarded the young hero, and even though their motives were pure, their campaign of criticism had its effect. Questions were raised about Jones's financial status and rumor abounded that he had amassed a fortune in treasure at the government's expense. Jones surprised his enemies by submitting personal accounts showing that he had not received a dollar of pay for his five years of service. When the American navy was temporarily abolished, Jones studied and wrote essays on naval tactics, a project which would later benefit many American seamen.

There was one last adventure left in America's famous naval commander. In 1785, he was persuaded by the Russian Empress Catherine II to serve as rear-admiral for her Black Sea fleet, then fighting the Turks. Some believed that Catherine the Great, attracted by the fame and gallantry of John Paul Jones, sent for him with plans of adding him to her staff of lovers, hoping that the much-traveled Scot-American romantic could fuse new emotions into her jaded life. That, at least, was the common gossip. In truth, she was trying to force the Turks out of Europe and gain an ice-free seaport open for her burgeoning empire. To accomplish this end, she needed an organized and competently commanded navy. Since she had no Russians with that reputation, Jones seemed the answer.

Before he left western Europe for the North Seas, and though he eagerly embraced the opportunity to acquire greater fame worldwide, the naval hero made it a point to write his friend, Thomas Jefferson, pledging his support of the emerging government. "This new constitution beyond question will create, when adopted by the necessary nine states, a firm and solid government. Its adoption assured not only by nine at once, but by all eventually..." He also wrote that he could "never renounce the glorious title of a citizen of the United States." Patriotism aside, vanity also played a major part in Jones's colorful persona. In another letter written as he departed for the Black Sea, having followed the advice of Jefferson to accept the commission, he described the opportunity. The project "opened up a vista of ambitious hopes and dreams of glory on a grand scale too powerful and vivid to be cast aside, and well worth the most careful consideration and deepest meditation."

Arriving in mysterious Russia, he was dazzled by Catherine. She instantly made him an equal of the Russian diplomats and superior of the most seasoned war veterans. He did play a successful part in several naval engagements, but due credit was never accorded him. Fellow officers and Catherine's own jealous lover saw to that. It seemed to be just another of many ironies and disillusionments. His only reward, despite the time of service, was the decoration of the Cross of the Order of St. Anne.

It was in Russia that the health of John Paul Jones began to decline. For much of his life he had experienced an assortment of ailments. Some could be attributed to the changes in diet and water, a by-product of his many travels. Now, far from home, the target of endless political schemes to discredit him, discouraged and sick, Jones was confined to bed for long periods.

In early 1789, as he rested in St. Petersburg, a Russian girl in her early teens came into the room and asked if he had any clothing for her to mend. According to his own account she, "began some earnest and indecent allurements of person." Jones "advised her to beware of such a career, gave her a ruble, and dismissed her." When he led her to the door, she raised an outcry and rushed into the street. She accused Jones of rape and screamed out the details to passersby. The girl, Catherine Koltzwarthen, and her procuress-mother, had successfully victimized others with the same scam. Under the circumstances, the traveler's innocence was understood, but some political enemies made much ado about "such an indecency."

The Russian years had been bitterly disappointing for Jones. With his usefulness ended and his reputation tainted, he was given a leave of absence and left for Paris. He was no longer the popular war hero — several years had passed since his brave deeds aboard the American ships. He left Russia a man without a country. The United States, in the midst of struggles to establish a stable government, could give him no employment. He had cut all ties to Scotland, the country of his birth. For obvious reasons, he could not involve himself with enemies of America, France, or Russia — too many downed sea vessels were remembered against him. France, although unable to use his services because of the approaching revolution, seemed his most logical stopping place.

In France, his health slowly declined. By the summer of 1792, he exhibited the serious symptoms of jaundice, kidney disease, and pneumonia. He lived in a friend's home on *Rue de Touron*, coughing fitfully, conversing often with admiring friends, and brooding over many tragic disappointments.

Thomas Jefferson sent a notice to him on June 1, detailing the hero's appointment by President George Washington as commissioner to Algiers, but he never received the message. On the night of July 18, 1792, alone, after reading one of Voltaire's works, Jones fell across his bed, face downward, swollen feet dangling on the floor. He never awakened. John Paul Jones, the man who in the heat of desperate battle had vowed, "I have not yet begun to fight!" had died. He was renowned for his courage under fire, for his determination in battle, for his refusal even to consider the option of surrender. He always persevered, but the torch burned out quickly. He was but 45 years of age at his death.

PERSEVERANCE

---

*"Any man can work when every stroke of
his hand brings down the fruit rattling
from the tree to the ground; but to labor in
season, under every discouragement, by
the power of truth — that requires a
heroism which is transcendent."*
— *Henry Ward Beecher*

Curiously, there is no college course on the subject of perseverance nor any textbook analyzing it. One can earn a degree in business, law, or science without ever having studied it. However, one cannot succeed, even in education, without knowing its power. Left to itself, any project, any dream, any marriage, any business will fail. Every enterprise will be challenged. Perseverance is that extra effort that takes one beyond the expected and the easy.

In discussions with great leaders who are worshipped as icons in their fields, they say that this is the principle that almost evaded them. The desire to stop, to give up, to walk away was a great temptation. Many have said that they did just that, and failed. However, when they came to the realization that quitting was no option, then failure was eliminated.

This is the most elusive of all the leadership attributes.

It is so easy to blame someone else for our lack of follow-through, simply because it is acceptable to many people. We, individually, are to blame for our failure to persevere. That things are too difficult, or we were not helped enough, flies in the face of those who have overcome greater obstacles than we.

"The man with the average mentality, but with control, with a definite goal, and a clear conception of how it can be gained, and above all, with the power of application and labor, wins in the end."
– William Howard

While we were toughened by the environment and hostile elements, Americans very quickly developed a stubborn sense of survival. Washington at Valley Forge, Jefferson in his persistent campaign to establish the University of Virginia, Franklin in his endless scientific experiments which ended in failure more often than not, are all examples of what Calvin Coolidge described as the "most important principle of success."

When ordered by German officers to surrender, the American commander at Bastogne during World War II, General McAuliffe, sent back the simple message, "Nuts." John Paul Jones shouted over the din of battle words that have become part of our American personality, "I have not yet begun to fight." For any leader, for any one person's

129

quest for success, that American spirit of winning, of stubborn perseverance, must be appropriated.

"An invincible determination can accomplish almost anything and in this lies the great distinction between great men and little men."
— Thomas Fuller

Chapter Five

Thomas Jefferson - Assuming Responsibility

"For the support of this Declaration, with a firm reliance on the protection of Divine Providence, we mutually pledge to each other our Lives, our Fortunes, and our sacred Honor." – Thomas Jefferson

Anton Signorile describes the typical American pilgrim as a very independent, almost defiant personality. Since the pilgrim was motivated by religious zeal, there was a self-righteousness that gave them strength. "Should we obey man rather than God?" Saint Peter once asked. The pilgrim had his answer. And yet, both Signorile and the political observer, de Tocqueville, speak of a great American "patriotism" born out of a sense of common responsibility. How could the new American be both independent and responsible to each other at the same time?

Once more the answer may lay in the environment. The hostile elements, the dangers of Indians and wild beasts, the remoteness which precluded quick or timely resupply of tools, guns, seeds or information all drew the independent American colonists together, forcing a common sense of mutual responsibility. As religious people, this instinct was naturally spiritual. Duty to God, to the station of marriage, to one's children all grew to become synonymous with duty to country. What may simply have been a necessity was canonized as a virtue.

133

> *"The brave man inattentive to his duty, is worth little more to his country than the coward who deserts her in the hour of danger." – Andrew Jackson*

Once again, America is unique in this respect, for while every nation and people have at times invoked God's "anointing" for war or other great undertakings, none go so far as to name Him in their constitution or on their money, let alone claim His "natural laws" as the basis for their existence. "We hold these truths to be self-evident: that all men are created equal, that they are endowed by their Creator with certain unalienable rights..."

And so, there is this paradox; that while the American personality is fiercely independent, to the point of boldness and brashness, it is also mutually caring of all the other brash, bold, independent, conspirators in this experiment in democracy. There is no complete explanation of the success of America without discussing this prominent feature. Patriotism, community responsibility, teamwork, a sense of duty; it is all part of the phenomena. America would never have been great without it. And while there are many great Americans who embody this principle, none were more reluctant, less suited to public life, than Thomas Jefferson. Only this sense of "patriotism" and community responsibility could have drawn him out. His life typifies the principle.

There is a common theme running throughout the stories of George Washington, John Hancock and Thomas Jefferson. Each man could have led a life of privileged ease. They need only support the Crown and the very socioeconomic system that had brought their families such success. It was simply a question of maintaining the status quo.

Washington's family owned lands. Hancock, through the largesse of his uncle, had money. Thomas Jefferson was born to both. Washington would become famous for his integrity and character, Hancock for his boldness and courage. Thomas Jefferson would become famous for giving birth to a better, more equitable system. For years, the monarchies that had subjugated and restricted the liberties of the masses had favored his own privileged family. Eventually, someone in some new generation would have to right the wrongs and remake the system. Thomas Jefferson was the man to assume that responsibility. While Washington's strength won the battles and Hancock's boldness inspired public support, Jefferson patiently devised a new, revolutionary form of government to replace the old. It was one thing to criticize, it was something altogether different to create.

Early Responsibilities

Jefferson was born on April 13, 1743, in Shadwell, Virginia. His father, Peter Jefferson was a prominent plantation owner with excellent ties to the Crown. His mother, Jane Randolph, was a descendant of one of England's most famous and powerful families of nobility. In past generations, the Randolphs had sometimes vied for the Crown themselves. Thomas Jefferson enjoyed a privileged childhood, with every educational opportunity. He was an accomplished violinist, artist, and very early began to demonstrate his talent for writing.

At the age of fourteen, all childhood joys came to an abrupt halt. Thomas Jefferson's father died. It would be another curious pattern he would share with Washington and Hancock. Indeed, many rebels, both good and bad, from Hitler to Mao Tse-Tung, have experienced the early death of a father, a phenomenon which causes endless debate among psychologists.

With the death of Peter Jefferson came tremendous responsibilities for the son. Thomas was left with the task of overseeing a vast family estate totaling 3,000 acres and hundreds of slaves. Most assumed that he would now drop his studies and devote himself full-time to managing the tobacco fields and the family finances. But Thomas Jefferson's thirst for knowledge would not allow it. At the age of seventeen, he was admitted to the College of William and Mary in Williamsburg, Virginia.

A Virginia Gentleman

Williamsburg, at the time the capital of Virginia, was a bustling town of one thousand. It was at William and

Mary that Thomas Jefferson met a professor who would change his life forever. William Small, a Scotsman who taught natural philosophy, awakened in Jefferson a great thirst for learning. Small became a surrogate father as well, teaching the young Virginian the art and responsibility of the life of a gentleman. It was among Small's friends in town, off campus, that Thomas Jefferson would meet other men who would greatly influence the course of his life.

George Wythe, a prominent legal scholar and member of the Virginia House of Burgesses, eventually became Jefferson's closest friend. And Francis Fauquier, the governor of Virginia, would make a lasting impression. The governor was impressed with the tall, shy youth from Shadwell. Jefferson was invited to play his violin at make-shift concerts at the governor's mansion. Very quickly, the education Jefferson began receiving at the governor's dinner table transcended anything taught at William and Mary. Years later, Jefferson wrote to a nephew explaining the influence of such gentlemen. He said quite frequently that often he didn't know which course was the right one to take, but if he would just imagine Mr. Wythe or the governor in the same situation, he knew at once what they would do.

Inspired by the integrity, the mature sense of responsibility, and the modesty of these accomplished men, Jefferson decided to pursue a career in law. On the surface, it was not a profession which best matched his personality. Despite his quiet, retiring manner, his exquisite gift of writing helped propel him quickly to the top of the Virginia legal world. As a lawyer, Jefferson became well-known throughout Virginia. In 1769, the same year that John

Hancock was first elected to the Massachusetts House, twenty-six-year-old Thomas Jefferson was elected to the Virginia House of Burgesses. He was fast becoming like one of the very men he had so admired as a youth.

In the House of Burgesses, Jefferson found himself an ally with a diverse cultural mix of talented Virginians all advocating greater independence from the rule of the mother country. There was a gentleman farmer, sometime soldier by the name of George Washington, who had won distinction and praise for his role in the French and Indian War. There was a passionate young advocate by the name of Richard Henry Lee. And finally, there was the eloquent Patrick Henry, already a sensation. Patrick Henry's speeches attracted large audiences and inspired or angered, depending on the bias of the listener. For awhile, Henry's popularity seemed to tower over the quiet, shy Thomas Jefferson, but eventually the written word outdistanced the spoken word, and the latter's skill as a writer began to show itself. The exquisite reasoning and mature wisdom of Jefferson's essays on the current controversies began to provoke interest and admiration all across the Virginia colony. Travelers from the countryside who were finally introduced to the prolific Thomas Jefferson were amazed at his youth.

Jefferson's quiet style did not help him much with women. At 6'3", he was a giant for his time and extremely shy and awkward, self-conscious about his gangly appearance and fiery red hair. After several emotionally bruising failures at romance, Jefferson struck up a friendship with a twenty-two-year-old widow by the name of Martha Weyles Skelton.

At first there was no hint at a romance; they were just friends who happened to share the same music teacher. In time, Jefferson and Mrs. Skelton spent long hours playing music together—she on the harpsichord and he on the violin, supposedly practicing for various concerts around town. The important difference between Martha Skelton and Jefferson's other friends of the fair sex was his level of self-confidence. Hiding behind his violin, Jefferson felt comfortable around her. Martha, who had read the young man's provocative essays, was not deceived by his apparent shyness and ineptitude with women. The couple were married on January 1, 1772, and they soon settled into Thomas Jefferson's unfinished dream house, Monticello.

The Reasonable Revolution

Shortly after Jefferson's marriage, the crisis between England and her American colonies began to heat up considerably. Jefferson was in the House of Burgesses when the meeting was interrupted with the astonishing news of the Boston Tea Party and the severe reaction taken by the Crown. It was an exhilarating time for Jefferson, both in his public life and at home. That summer, his wife gave birth to their daughter, Martha. Two years later their daughter Jane would be born. Meanwhile, an essay he had written outlining the principles behind Virginia's support of her sister colony of Massachusetts was enthusiastically promoted by radical Virginians. It was printed under the title *A Summary View of the Rights of British America,* and widely disseminated throughout the thirteen colonies.

Jefferson's *Summary View* was a bombshell, condemned by moderates and embraced with excitement by the so-called patriots. With his now finely honed skill as a political writer, and drawing on his background as an attorney, Jefferson wove a dispassionate moral and legal argument suggesting that the British Parliament had forfeited its control over the colonies. This booklet was sent along to the Continental Congress by a Virginia committee in 1774. Members of Congress were impressed by Jefferson's work, and subsequently, the thirty-one-year-old lawyer-tobacco plantation owner was asked to join them in Philadelphia.

Thomas Jefferson's vision was considered much too radical by many of his contemporaries. When he submitted a constitution for the Commonwealth of Virginia, most of the ideas were discarded. Jefferson's passionate ideas about freeing the slaves, guaranteeing religious liberty in a colony that was exclusively Church of England, and granting every citizen the right to vote, were not even kept for discussion. But his arguments challenging the authority of King George and the British parliament were enthusiastically embraced. No one could better articulate the moral and legal rationale for the colonial resistance.

Jefferson engaged little in the great debates of the Continental Congress, but again and again he was called upon to write up the summaries of their conclusions. There was a bit of politics behind the assignment. Virginia, with its rich tobacco crop and its close ties to the English mother country, was a critical ally for the patriots. Massachusetts could not oppose England alone. Continually, the Continental Congress turned to George Washington, Thomas Jefferson and other Virginians, hoping that loyal Virginians following the proceedings back home would develop a sense of pride and participation in the events. Ultimately, many of the documents generated by the Congress began to reflect Jefferson's views. It was a subtle process, but one which was wryly noticed by America's most famous sage, Benjamin Franklin.

When the time came to declare colonial independence, and to do so on paper, the Congress once again turned to Thomas Jefferson. But the youthful Virginian was weary. He had watched the ferocious debate among the colonists and knew that such an assignment would be a thankless, if not impossible task. He convinced the Congress to give the job to the distinguished and able John Adams of Massachusetts, who promptly sent the project back to Jefferson. "He is a better writer than I am," Adams said, "And besides he is from Virginia."

It took Thomas Jefferson two-and-a-half weeks to finish the first draft of the Declaration of Independence. When the document was presented to the Congress on June 28, 1776, it was ripped to shreds by the members. Jefferson, with his pride of authorship on the line, simmered as his friend John Adams argued in defense of the document. Once more, Jefferson's words on slavery would have to go. Still, some of the most eloquent themes, Jefferson's moral *rasion d'etre* for the new country, survived the revisions of the Continental Congress. Indeed, his *"reason for existence*" had survived the ages and has been quoted by freedom fighters in South America, Asia, Africa and Europe.

A passage from Jefferson's opening paragraph is memorized by today's school children: "We hold these truths to be self-evident: that all men are created equal, that they are endowed by their Creator with certain unalienable rights, that among these are life, liberty, and the pursuit of happiness. That to secure these rights, governments are instituted among men, deriving their just powers from the consent of the governed; that whenever any form of government becomes destructive of these ends, it is the right of the people to alter or to abolish it, and to institute new government, laying its foundation on such principles and organizing its powers in such form, as to them shall seem most likely to effect their safety and happiness."

It was a stunning moment and everyone knew it. Both the act and the statement itself would reverberate across the world and down through the ages. Before the night of July 4, 1776, printed copies of the document began issuing out of Philadelphia. By the next morning, they started appearing on town hall bulletin boards across the thirteen colonies. Before the end of the month, Jefferson's words would be translated into dozens of languages and studied with amazement in Paris, Warsaw, Madrid, The Hague and across Europe. What had these Americans done? Never before had a revolution been declared with such moral dignity. The stamp of Thomas Jefferson, Virginia lawyer, architect, philosopher and tobacco plantation owner, was upon it.

The Death of a Dream

After the exciting days of the Continental Congress, Thomas Jefferson returned to his beloved Monticello where he fully expected to live a tranquil life as a gentleman tobacco planter. He and Martha had great plans for their estate. However, the events in Philadelphia had changed his life forever. He and his words were famous. The War for Independence was raging. His fellow Virginian, George Washington, was leading the army in battles fought in Massachusetts, Connecticut and New York. Every man and every talent was needed.

In June 1779, Jefferson was chosen as Virginia's new governor. It was to be a painful experience. When British troops invaded Virginia and took the capital, Jefferson and his cabinet fled. Brave colonists were outraged at the "cowardice." Jefferson, the man who would become famous for assuming responsibility, regardless of the circumstances or its personal price, resigned after only two years, leaving the post to a military governor. He wrote later that the experience had left "a wound on his spirit" that would only be cured by the grave.

Once more Jefferson retreated to Monticello where he wrote *Notes on the State of Virginia,* a lesson in the geography and politics of the state. Portions of the book were used in the drafting of a new Virginia Constitution. But with the completion of this work, the world of war and politics began to fade rapidly from his mind. Jefferson

143

continually rejected all appointments and positions which were tendered. When George Washington accepted the surrender of British General Cornwallis in October 1781, and Jefferson's friends insisted that he come help in the exciting work of creating a new nation, Jefferson expressed little interest. That part of his life was over. To his wife, Martha, who had grown resentful of the demands of his public life, he promised years devoted to the completion of his dream, now their dream, the estates at Monticello. Jefferson seemed to take great pleasure in his domestic life, supervising the education of his daughters, and building new barns.

Thomas and Martha had seen three of their other children die in infancy, including a son who had lived only seventeen days. Fortunately, Martha soon became pregnant again, and on May 8, 1782, the Jefferson's welcomed their third surviving child, Lucy Elizabeth, into their lives. It was a great moment for the family. The famous father who had often been away was now committed to life on the plantation. His daughters were thriving with his fatherly attention. However, after giving birth six times in ten years, Martha Jefferson's health was failing.

Both husband and wife now sensed that if Martha could recover, these would be the happiest years of their life together. During these weeks, when Jefferson learned that he had been elected to the Virginia legislature without his knowledge or approval, he angrily refused to go. It was one thing for friends to lecture him on his responsibility to the state; it was something altogether different for the state to make slaves of its own citizens. For months after the birth of Lucy, Martha struggled to live. Jefferson, a concerned husband, hovered over her, whispering his love, making his promises. Yet on the morning of September 6, 1782, Martha Skelton Jefferson passed away.

Much has been written of Thomas Jefferson's inconsolable grief at the loss of his wife. There were long months of insomnia, of lonely midnight rides along seldom used trails and roads. Jefferson burned every letter the two of them had written to each other, as if the romance were too sacred for anyone else to intrude upon. He was thirty-nine-years-old that fall morning when Martha died.

A French Renaissance

Jefferson's time of grieving evidently became a time of self-examination as well. Never again would he deny a request from his country. When the Continental Congress asked him to join John Adams and Benjamin Franklin as their representatives to Paris, he readily accepted. He expected to stay two years, just enough time to conclude a series of commercial treaties between the two countries. However, he would remain in France for five tumultuous years filled with international intrigue and diplomacy. On July 5, 1784, Thomas Jefferson sailed for France, taking with him his oldest daughter, his violin, and a copy of *Notes on the State of Virginia*. In Paris, he moved from place to place, searching for a house that captured some of the atmosphere of his beloved Monticello. Next to Benjamin

Franklin, Thomas Jefferson became the most popular American in France, constantly invited to dinners and balls, and often invited as a special celebrity guest for discussion groups, then the rage on the continent.

It was through these friendships that Jefferson met Maria Cosway, an Italian who had immigrated to England and was living briefly in Paris with her husband. It was rumored that her marriage was one of convenience and was a rather unhappy one. Jefferson secretly courted her. When she left France for London, he sent her what was to become a much celebrated letter entitled, "A dialogue between my head and my heart." Over the years it has become one of history's most famous and cherished love letters, but even beyond revealing Jefferson's unconsummated love affair, it offers historians an insightful glimpse of the personal pain and price Jefferson paid for his newfound sense of public responsibility. Jefferson conquered the passions of his heart, committed himself to his duties of state, and ended the affair.

Modern Americans must find it a bit confusing that at such a critical time, the young United States would send to Europe three of its most talented leaders, Benjamin Franklin, John Adams and Thomas Jefferson. In Philadelphia, the nation's capital at that point, a new constitution was being debated and the very foundations of the Republic were being formed. The survival of the new nation depended on diplomatic recognition, foreign investment capital, loans, and some accommodation with the powerful British Empire. Though Britain had seen its Royal Expeditionary Force defeated by General

Washington, it still ruled the waves. In many respects, the drama playing out in London and Paris was more critical to America's future than the drama in Philadelphia.

Though thousands of miles away, with critical work to do for his nation's survival, Jefferson was regularly consulted for his views on the new Constitution. A voluminous correspondence began with James Madison which shows the extent of Jefferson's contributions to the document. With his new sense of responsibility, there was no issue which Jefferson ignored or left to chance. When he received the final draft of the document, he gave his reluctant approval, but warned that some basic principles guiding the relationship between the government and its people were missing. Jefferson suggested that they add a "Statement of Individual Rights" to spell out the liberties of the people and to shield them from any future oppression. Such a "Statement" should be issued jointly with the Constitution. Jefferson became increasingly convinced of the necessity of such a document, raising the ante by suggesting that it be an addendum to the Constitution itself. Eventually, because of Jefferson's pressure, The Bill of Rights was passed. The reasonableness and moral strength of this document reflects the Jeffersonian style. Throughout history, it has become the model for scores of free states emerging from corrupt monarchies, totalitarianism, and dictatorships.

One of those states emerging from a corrupt monarchy was France itself. In March of 1779, emboldened by the America experience, the French legislative assembly issued its *Cahiers de dolances,* a list of grievances collected by the people. It called for a new constitution which would spell out the rights and liberties of each citizen and end the outdated feudal system which still dominated rural areas. As the American author of the Declaration of Independence and much of the now sensational Bill of Rights, Jefferson was earnestly sought out by French revolutionaries, including America's erstwhile friend, the Marquis de Lafayette. However, it was a time for caution. After all, Jefferson had been appointed as America's minister to the court of Versailles, seat of the French King, Louis XVI, whose loans had all but guaranteed American independence. Respectfully and with dignity, Jefferson explained to the emerging French radicals the reasoning behind America's Constitution and its Bill of Rights. France was about to explode and the French people who had sacrificed to help ensure American independence would eventually be the beneficiaries.

The Great Federalist Debate

In the midst of such dangerous and exciting times, Thomas Jefferson received word that under the new Constitution, which he had helped write, General George Washington had been elected the first President of the United States. As runner-up, his close friend, John Adams, had been elected vice president. Months later came the news that the new president had appointed him as the nation's first secretary of state. On September 26, 1789, after five years in Paris, a happy and flattered Thomas

Jefferson set sail for America, filled with excitement about his new assignment.

In Philadelphia, the nation's capital, Jefferson's euphoria soon disappeared. The work of running the country was not easy. Administrative work was tedious and offered little personal reward or sense of accomplishment. His successful negotiation of the so-called Pinckney's Treaty with Spain, was enthusiastically applauded by the country. This treaty permitted the United States to explore the Mississippi, which would ultimately lead to the expansion of American borders. The endless departmental intrigues and petty rivalries sapped his energy and happiness. More than once, Jefferson expressed his personal regret at having taken on the assignment, telling close friends that only a sense of "duty" to the people kept him going.

A much more serious challenge for Jefferson was the growing political rift in the nation. Treasury Secretary Alexander Hamilton was arguing in favor of a stronger federal government to keep order and help get the nation moving. Jefferson, who advocated the philosophy of free markets and taught "that government governs best which governs least," was appalled. Again and again he countered Hamilton's ideas, while privately expressing astonishment that no one else seemed willing to challenge this new threat to all they had accomplished. Within a short time, Hamilton and Jefferson's philosophical feud erupted publicly, with advocates taking sides and President Washington struggling to hold them both together.

When Vice President John Adams, Jefferson's old friend, sided with Alexander Hamilton, the issue turned personal. Alarmed by Hamilton's bandwagon, Jefferson organized a series of meetings with political allies. The nation was soon rent by the great partisan debate. Hamilton and Adams organized a political party, calling themselves the Federalists. Jefferson and Madison founded another political party, calling themselves the Republicans. John Adams and Thomas Jefferson, once inseparable colleagues who had argued and fought for American independence, were now bitter political enemies.

The Third President

When George Washington grandly decided not to run for a third term as president, the partisan split became more serious than ever. The Federalists nominated John Adams. The Republicans nominated Thomas Jefferson. Adams won the vote in the electoral college by only three votes, making Jefferson the new vice president, serving with a man whose political philosophy he openly despised.

It was during the presidency of John Adams that the nation's capital was moved to Washington, D.C., and the White House became the president's new official residence. At that time, America was close to war with France; ironically, the country who helped guarantee her freedom.

Not surprisingly, Adams and Jefferson had completely different views on nearly everything, including the French Revolution. Angered over American refusal to help them in their revolution, the new radical French government had begun attacking American vessels on the high seas. President Adams called for America to retaliate, to take a stand against such aggression. Jefferson admitted that the Revolution was out of hand, but felt America should avoid going to war with the very people who had helped her win her independence.

During the debate, Adams proposed negotiations with the French, sending ministers to France to seek an agreement. The American representatives were told by three French diplomats, known only as "X", "Y", and "Z", that the French would negotiate a treaty if the Americans would bribe the French foreign minister, Charles Maurice de Talleyrand-Perigord. The astonished Americans promptly ended the negotiations, returned to the United States, and President John Adams told the American people to prepare for war.

Some in the Federalist Party were growing weary of the president's caution. When French Foreign Minister Talleyrand, frightened by the prospect of an Anglo-American war with France sent signals that a second negotiating team for the United States would have a better reception, Adams sent his ministers back to Paris. War was averted, but leaders in Adam's own political party, the Federalists, were in an uproar.

In an attempt to keep their political party alive, Federalists in Congress passed the Alien and Sedition Acts. This legislation allowed the president to deport any foreigner he believed to be dangerous. Furthermore, these Acts gave the president broad power to prosecute any publisher printing libelous material about any government employee.

151

Jefferson believed that these acts were unconstitutional. He also knew fighting against the legislation was a sure way to rally public opinion against the Federalists. He teamed up with James Madison, and together they wrote the Kentucky and Virginia Resolutions, giving the states the right to decide when an act of Congress is unconstitutional.

Ultimately, Jefferson and Madison's Resolutions were not needed to destroy the Federalist party. The Federalists did the job themselves, splitting the party after the signing of the peace treaty with France. Federalists in both camps envisioned victory for their respective candidates, but some observers could smell an upset. When the electoral votes were finally counted, the Republicans had won in a landslide. But there was a tie between their two most popular figures, controversial firebrand Aaron Burr and the sitting vice president, Thomas Jefferson. According to the Constitution, the decision of who would be president and who would be vice president would be passed on to the House of Representatives.

It took thirty-six ballots for the House to make up its mind. In the end, divided Federalists repelled by the campaign rhetoric of Aaron Burr, threw their support to the man from Monticello. Burr's old nemesis, Treasury Secretary Alexander Hamilton, was especially influential. Though Jefferson was despised by radicals in both parties for his attempts at personal reconciliation, he was considered by the Federalists as the lesser of two evils. And so it was that John Adams left the White House and his old friend and now bitter enemy, Thomas Jefferson, moved in. The man who had twice retired from politics, vowing that he would never come back, was now President of the United States.

America Doubles Its Size

The so-called "Jeffersonian Revolution" was a huge success. The power of governing was given exclusively to the people, and basic rights of the citizens were reaffirmed. At first, his moves were bitterly resisted by Federalists in Congress who warned that Jefferson was dismantling the government, and that the country could not survive the changes. Alexander Hamilton warned that the treasury would cease to function and the nation would go bankrupt. Within time, the new president was able to establish a truce between Federalists and Republicans. Jefferson kept promoting nonpartisan cooperation. If Federalists and Republicans work together, he would say, both will benefit.

Considering his political philosophy, Jefferson would use his executive powers with great decisiveness and strength when the occasion so merited. After a very speedy and forceful negotiation which ignored Congress and bypassed his old department of state, Jefferson concluded the Louisiana Purchase. For the price of $15 million, the United States was more than doubling its territory. The great land sale prompted an uproar among Washington politicians, including many in Jefferson's own political party, who considered the president's secret actions unconstitutional. Federalists were outraged by the price tag. Others questioned the political wisdom of the deal. Was America only financing the wars of Napoleon Bonaparte?

The American people, however, were delirious with excitement. Most could already see the wisdom of the decision. Overnight, the port city of New Orleans had become the largest city in the young nation. Within the first few weeks some settlers began heading west. Jefferson, thrilled by the prospect of learning more about the region, immediately dispatched a team of surveyors and scientists to explore its furthest limits. In the spring of 1804, Captain William Clark and Merriweather Lewis began an exciting journey, which in three months, would take them to the Pacific Ocean. Americans followed the adventure with avid interest. In 1804, buoyed by his great foreign policy successes, Thomas Jefferson was reelected president in a landslide.

In the midst of Jefferson's successful campaign of 1804, the seeds were sown for a very personal, bitter drama that would distract from the president's second term and ultimately poison it. Following the controversial election of 1800, in which the decision of who would be president had been passed onto the House of Representatives, the Constitution was changed so that presidents and vice presidents would be elected in tandem, as a team, a ticket. Jefferson promptly announced that he would be dropping the controversial Aaron Burr as his vice presidential running mate, favoring instead his old friend, James Madison. A Republican convention affirmed the decision. Burr was out.

Not every region of the country, however, was completely happy with the president from Monticello. New Englanders were growing furious with the perceived French tilt in Jefferson's foreign policy. Their ties were with the British, who spoke the same language and who represented their greatest market for produced goods. A very small but powerful group of New England merchants and politicians had been advocating secession. They had tried cultivating the great Jefferson antagonist, Alexander Hamilton, as an ally. If they had his support, they explained, New England could declare independence from the United States and Hamilton could lead them. The former treasury secretary and leading Federalist rebuffed them. Now, Aaron Burr, a national figure and the current sitting vice president and rival of Thomas Jefferson, was returning to his home in New York. Yes, he was a Republican, but that made it even sweeter. Talks began with Aaron Burr.

In 1804, while the ticket of Thomas Jefferson and James Madison was winning the national election, Aaron Burr, the current vice president, was locked in a bitter contest for governor of New York. In the course of the campaign, his old nemesis, Alexander Hamilton, exposed the secessionist's plot. The Burr campaign went down in flames.

On July 11, 1804, Thomas Jefferson was in the White House when he learned, along with a shocked nation, that his vice president, Aaron Burr, had pumped two bullets into the former secretary of the treasury, Alexander Hamilton. The most celebrated political and personal feud in the country was over, and with it, the political career of the vice president. The duel, which had been perfectly legal in New Jersey, resulted in the death of Hamilton. The nation was outraged.

Meanwhile, an angry Aaron Burr fled south where he began recruiting a small army. History is still ignorant of his scheme, though most suggest he was planning an invasion of Mexico or plotting a move to declare Louisiana as an independent state. Jefferson had him arrested and tried for treason. Burr was acquitted and fled to Europe. He would later return to the United States under an assumed name, but his public career was at an end.

Anxious to get the bizarre and debilitating Burr affair behind him, Jefferson turned to foreign policy where he had experienced such spectacular success in his first term. The ongoing rivalry between Great Britain and France was now having a serious impact on American exports. The British ports refused ships that had previously visited French ports and the French ports refused ships that had previously visited Great Britain. In a grand display of statesmanship, Jefferson proposed an embargo on both nations. It had worked well during the Revolution. Perhaps it would bring these two stubborn superpowers to the negotiating table. The Embargo Act passed the House and Senate. America was officially neutral.

However, it was not the British and the French who suffered under the Embargo Act. It was the American merchants and manufacturers. If Jefferson's great show-piece of the first administration, the Louisiana Purchase, had been such an obvious success, likewise, the Embargo Act of the second term was an obvious disaster. Under pressure, Jefferson backed down and the Act was repealed by the Senate.

A Friend Once More

After serving his second term, Thomas Jefferson reaffirmed the tradition started by George Washington and stepped down from the presidency. After a lifetime of public service, he had fulfilled his responsibility to the people and had kept his own personal vow. The baton was passed to his vice president, James Madison, and Thomas Jefferson finally retired to his beloved Monticello.

Satisfied that his public career was over, Jefferson plunged into his retirement with zest. For the first time since his short childhood, he could relax. He read from his library, worked in his gardens, rode his horses, visited with neighbors, and continued enlarging Monticello.

Only one project lured him from his peaceful retirement. Years before, he had urged the State of Virginia to establish an educational system open to all, regardless of income or breeding. Now, when no one else was willing to take on the project, Jefferson took matters into his own hands, planning and founding the University of Virginia.

There was one matter left unfinished. In 1812, he renewed his friendship with his long lost companion, John Adams. They had worked side by side during the American Revolution. They had served in George Washington's administration together. Both had been vice presidents.

157

Both had been presidents. But political rivalry and philosophical differences had made them bitter enemies. Now in retirement, Jefferson assumed the responsibility to resolve the feud. In a massive exchange of letters over a period of many years, the two lonely men, far from the seat of power, renewed their friendship and respect for each other.

By 1826, Jefferson's health was failing. Family and friends knew that there was only one thing keeping him alive, his desire to see the 50th anniversary of the Declaration of Independence. On the night of July 3rd, he fell seriously ill. At midnight he stirred and asked one of his servants if the Fourth had arrived. When told that it had, he fainted on the spot and died a few minutes later.

Meanwhile, several thousand miles away, a similar scene was being played out at the home of John Adams. Only a few hours after Jefferson passed away, John Adams rose from his sleep and uttered his final words: "Thomas Jefferson still lives." And so it was, that on the Fourth of July, America's birthday, two of America's greatest presidents passed into the pages of history.

Architect, farmer, musician, lawyer, Thomas Jefferson forfeited his many interests and personal pleasures to serve the people. More than a hundred years later, John Kennedy would remind Americans to "ask not what your country can do for you, but ask rather, what you can do for your country." It is part of the American formula. While the citizens of many societies wait for their government to lead them, take care of them, and decide for them, the spirit of an American is one of independent responsibility. "Duty and responsibility," Jefferson taught, "were the obligation of every citizen in a free society."

RESPONSIBILITY

> *"You can't escape the responsibility of tomorrow by evading it today."*
> *– Abraham Lincoln*

Applying the American leadership principles to your personal life must include this caveat: no one's personal success, to be honored, can come at the expense of your marriage or children. True and lasting success will involve "doing what is right," even if it seems like a detour for the moment. Duty comes before profit.

It is true that some people seem to achieve while seemingly disregarding this principle. We have elected public servants and cheered athletes who are often forgiven for their lack of responsibility. Some chief executives of large companies seem to be rewarded for their pursuit of profit at the expense of people. While in some situations they are acting responsibly to their shareholders, there are many examples where they are not.

> *"Where are our men of abilities, why do they not come forth to save their country."*
> *– George Washington*

This principle, coupled with the last of our leadership principles are the two most important. While Americans avidly cherish "individual rights," we have developed a sense of duty almost akin to the Prussian military ethic— the great difference being that the Prussian culture demanded it, while the American culture appeals out of a sense of fairness and right. It was this same sense of responsibility that caused Washington to return to public life when he was longing to retire. It was the same for Franklin. This sense of responsibility was the driving force in Jefferson's personality. Hancock was willing to lose everything he owned for the greater community good. Jones refused to run, even from a certain defeat.

Time and again, the United States has taken on a cause or a fight that was not ours, simply to right a wrong or correct an injustice. This has sometimes led to misunderstanding and resentment by other nations, as well as by citizens of our own. However, responsibility is one of the primary attributes of honorable leadership that we, as a nation and as individuals, must uphold.

"Those who expect to reap the blessing of freedom, must, like men, undergo the fatigue of supporting it." – Thomas Paine

---

Chapter Six

George Washington - Leading with Character

"I hope I shall possess firmness and virtue enough to maintain what I consider the most enviable of all titles, the character of an 'Honest Man.'"
– George Washington

Today, when a lawsuit is filed every six minutes, Americans speak fondly of an earlier time when a man's word was his bond. Integrity was crucial to survival in a frontier society. There were few courts of law and no state police for enforcement. A contract was often a simple handshake.

Some scholars attribute this ideal of early America to its religious beginnings. Pious puritan pilgrims took their faith seriously. In early Jamestown, the telling of a lie resulted in a weekend in the stocks. Other scholars invoke an anecdotal theory that colonists were embittered by their cavalier and high-handed treatment by their mother country, England. "The government has lied to us again," was the bitter, if naive colonists' refrain. Of course, as the famous British prime minister Benjamin Disraeli once pointed out, "all governments are liars." Few have the institutional memory to maintain any degree of integrity in internal operations, let alone in service to its citizens. But early colonists had little governmental experience with which to compare. As far as they were concerned, the English Crown had misled them and repeatedly broken its promises.

While this resulted in some hardship for English citizens at home, in the wilds of the American frontier, it was sometimes an issue of life and death. On the frontier, one's life depended on keeping one's word. If the American colonists were represented in Parliament, or better yet free, they would show the way. Government must first be honest, or it is worth nothing at all.

"Nearly all men can stand adversity, but if you want to test a man's character, give him power." – Abraham Lincoln

---

Over the years, this naive piece of American common sense has remade itself in many wondrous and various ways, and like almost everything else American, has been commercialized. "The customer is always right," is a truly American manifestation. Today, department stores in modern France are considered revolutionary for remaining open until 9:00 P.M., the week before Christmas. American malls do it every night. Walt Disney World, where the attitudes of employees are seemingly maintained on an even keel with a thermostat, may be the ultimate expression of this "desire to please the people." America's first and most legendary example of a life of character, indeed of honesty personified, is the story of George Washington.

A Life in the Wilderness

Washington's story is our fifth and last American profile illustrating the "American philosophy." The apocryphal story which has him admitting to his father, "I cannot tell a lie. I was the one who chopped down your cherry tree," was used for 150 years as a lesson to teach each succeeding generation of American youth that honesty is an essential ingredient to any successful life.

Born February 11, 1732, to Augustine Washington and Mary Ball, George, from early childhood, participated in the insular life of a middle income planter family as the family moved to a series of farms on the Rappahannock and Potomac Rivers.

Though accepted as a "Virginia gentleman," George Washington was earthier, more practical, more ambitious, and much tougher than the sanitized version offered up to today's grade school children. The Washington household was guided by English manners, but the family lived dangerously close to the wilderness. As was the case of many mid-to-upper class Virginians, they were land-rich and money-poor. The lack of money seemed to motivate young George to dream, to want more than a status-quo existence.

His education was short and haphazard, and he was largely self-taught. At sixteen he left his family to become a surveyor's assistant on the rustic frontier lands owned by the wealthy friend of the family, Lord Fairfax. The once-genteel young man roughed it up in the wilderness, visiting Indian villages where he witnessed "naked savages in a demonic dancing frenzy," and where he caught "live fleas" from sleeping on a backwoodsman's verminous pallet. Such excursions only increased his youthful desire to gain wealth, land, and honor. Due to the family relationship with the prominent Lord Fairfax, Washington quickly developed the profitable trait of cultivating the attention and friendship of prominent men.

The French And Indian War

In July of 1752, French forces overran the English trading post of Pickawilly in the Ohio River Valley and the great Anglo-French rivalry that dominated Continental politics suddenly flashed into open conflict in North America. More alarming to the colonists was the fact that several Indian nations were enlisted to help the French. By the following spring, the threatened English colony of Virginia had organized a volunteer militia.

No one had a better knowledge of the territory than the twenty-one-year-old surveyor, George Washington, who through necessity had literally lived in the wild for months at a time. And so it was, through this coincidence, that Washington became Virginia's first commissioned officer. His improbable and spectacular career was launched.

Washington's early military record was one of great personal bravery offset by strategic and tactical failure. He accomplished little in 1753 other than a long march to Lake Erie, where he issued an ultimatum to the French at Fort Le Boeuf, reaffirming British claims to the Ohio River Valley region. The following spring, the governor of Virginia ordered Washington to take his regiment to the fork of the Allegheny and Monongahela Rivers, site of present day Pittsburgh, Pennsylvania, where he was to build a fort guarding the Ohio Valley. Washington completed the project after which the French promptly chased him away, occupying the new fort for themselves and capturing Washington's arms supply. In late summer, Washington's regimental army was ignominiously defeated by the French at Fort Necessity.

Yet, through it all, he became an American hero. Stories of his personal courage and his care for his men seemed to transcend any need for victory on the battlefield. He was America's soldier.

That personal courage had its ultimate test the following year when the great British General Edward Braddock arrived with one thousand crack British soldiers. Braddock had been sent to reclaim Washington's fort, which the French now christened Fort Dusquesne. Washington was to come along as a subordinate officer, or as one British writer suggested, "a glorified scout," and to get a lesson in soldiering.

Braddock's march and subsequent baptism into warfare American style, has been the subject of great ridicule by historians, but it was a deadly business. The French and Indians surprised the English army in an ambush, seven miles short of the fort. Suddenly, rising from the woods like ringwraithes in a J. R. R. Tolkien fantasy, the French and their painted Indian allies easily massacred the English soldiers, whose bright red coats made ready targets. More than seven hundred British soldiers lay dead, including Braddock himself.

With Braddock's death, command now fell on twenty-three-year-old Lieutenant Colonel George Washington who turned a disastrous rout into an organized, rapid retreat. In the melee, two horses were killed beneath him and four bullet holes were found in his coat. "The All-Powerful Providence," he wrote later, had protected him. It was, after all, one more defeat. However, nothing seemed to tarnish the image of the young man who would someday become American's first "teflon" president. George Washington was now more celebrated than ever.

As part of a protracted and larger conflict between France and England in Europe, the French and Indian War was, in fact, the longest in North American history. Lasting more than ten years, and ending with the Treaty of Paris in 1763, this conflict effectively ceded Canada and the Ohio Valley to England and her colonies.

Many soldiers, British, French and Colonial, seized the time to make their mark on military history. While young Washington failed to earn his laurels in this protracted war, the adventure did help refine his understanding of warfare, American style. To survive in the lush forests of the Eastern seaboard, one had to fight like an Indian. Washington learned that independent-minded American colonists made poor soldiers, unwilling to take orders unless everything was explained to them, an impossibility during the fluid events of a battlefield. Toward the end of the war,

Washington finally hardened. Two deserters were hung as examples. Only a disciplined army could hope to win, he realized. It was a lesson that would serve him well in the years ahead.

At the end of the French and Indian War, George Washington gave up his commission in the Virginia militia to marry Martha Custis, a rich widow and landowner. He would run Martha's farm and capitalize on his new found fame by seeking a seat in the Virginia House of Burgesses. He often wrote of these years as the best of his life. He relished the title, "farmer George."

Sixteen years later, independence fever rushed through the colonies and Washington was caught up in the excitement. He wrote about the "peaceful plains of America," emphasizing that they were "either to be drenched with blood or inhabited by slaves." Asked Washington, "Can a virtuous man hesitate in his choice?"

Leading the Continental Army

By June 13, 1775, when the Second Continental Congress created a new Continental army, it had become apparent that Washington would be recalled to military service to lead it into battle. After his record in the French and Indian War, no one could accuse George Washington of being a military genius, but he was courageous and popular. His appointment would make it easier to recruit volunteers. He did have experience, and more importantly to the colonial leaders who were rebelling against English "tyranny," Washington was a colleague of proven integrity. He would not abuse the power they were giving him.

The new Commander in Chief, a Virginia tobacco planter, publicly confessed that he "did not believe himself equal to the command," and at one point begged his colleagues to reconsider. He confided to Patrick Henry, "Remember, Mr. Henry, what I now tell you. From the day I enter upon the command of the American armies, I date my fall, and the ruin of my reputation." George Washington departed Philadelphia on June 23, 1775, and took up his command two weeks after the Battle of Bunker Hill.

The American War of Independence was not likely to offer a favorable outcome for the thirteen colonies. They were barely united in their decision to break with England and were bitterly feuding over the process. British sanctions had denied them any meaningful industry. Their men had little if any military experience; they had no navy, no army, few military supplies and no allies. Yes, they had thousands of frontiersmen who knew how to hunt for food and were not strangers to either guns or hardships, but on the other hand, they would be facing the most well-trained troops in the world.

Many other colonies had already tried what the thirteen colonies were now trying and had not succeeded. The British had already defeated armies ten times their size in such diverse and inhospitable lands as China, India, and Egypt. The thirteen American colonies, with their combined population of five million, could not hope to field armies the size of the Egyptians, Indians, and Chinese. The British knew how to adapt. They proved they could win anywhere against anybody. With its powerful navy, which controlled the world's sea lanes and its most important straits, the British could guarantee supply to its armies anywhere on earth and isolate anyone it wanted.

To complicate matters further, most American Indian tribes were lining up on the British side, meaning that much needed troops would be required to guard frontier outposts and protect citizens. Yet the greatest cause for concern was the large loyalist population, the Tories, those American colonists who sided with the Crown and were willing to fight, spy, or work to help the English motherland. Some were only opportunists, betting on the horse that was likely to win, and thus hoping to reap the good fortune that would follow. Others were frightened by the ominous odds. But some were morally repulsed by the idea of rebellion. They reasoned this was Lucifer's great sin. What civilization countenanced such a thing?

On July 4, 1776, the United States of America declared independence. Euphoria swept the thirteen colonies. There was no turning back. Sometime in the next few months or years, George Washington would either be hanged in a public square or feted as the leader of a new nation.

That winter, British General Lord Cornwallis led a huge contingent of twelve regiments into battle against Washington's Continental army camped in nearby New Jersey. Washington had little choice but to scamper across the Delaware River to safety, abandoning New Jersey. But two weeks later he would strike back. Borrowing a tactic that he had seen the Indians use to great effect in the French and Indian War, Washington planned a surprise hit-and-run raid across the river. Cornwallis had left two regiments of Hessian mercenaries behind to watch Washington's army till spring, but no one expected to hear anything from them.

As winter deepened, Washington's regulars dwindled to 2400 men. On December 20, 1776, the commander wrote to Congress, "Ten more days will put an end to the existence of our army." The young nation's morale had never been lower.

On the night of Christmas Eve, December 24, 1776, while the nearby Hessian soldiers were sleeping off their feasting and celebration, Washington took a desperate gamble. For six hours, throughout the darkness, he moved his army of 2400 soldiers across the treacherous, icy Delaware River in small boats, ferrying back and forth. A howling snowstorm provided a natural screen.

On Christmas morning, when Washington's army finally assembled and the order to attack had been given, the Hessians were totally surprised. One hundred men were gunned down on the spot, including the Hessian commander. More than 900 were taken prisoner. Like phantoms, Washington's army disappeared into the darkness back across the Delaware, taking their prisoners, six German brass cannons, and tons of desperately needed supplies. Two American soldiers froze to death; they were Washington's only casualties.

The colonies were electrified. Bells rang from church steeples across the country. The American Commander in

Chief and his heroic army were cheered. Washington, who was already loved and respected in the colonies, was now an international hero, talked about in the salons of France and Prussia where the American War of Independence was finally attracting some attention.

The Surrender of Cornwallis

Washington's celebrated New Jersey raid became the pattern that would be repeated throughout the War. Defeat after defeat would bring the Continental army to the edge of annihilation, whereupon a bold, usually strategically unimportant Washington counter stroke would rally them from despair. In January 1777, following his victory over the Hessians, his army defeated British regulars in Princeton.

Yet such victories on the battlefield were rare. With a superior British army in the field and with a powerful British fleet guarding each harbor, Washington's small forces soon found themselves isolated. In the fall, British troops occupied Philadelphia, the young nation's capital.

During the next winter, resupply suddenly became more urgent than any tactical maneuver on the battlefield. Now, they were facing an enemy more relentless than the English. Starvation and disease, brought on by malnutrition, spread through the ranks. Life at the winter quarters in Valley Forge became a grotesque nightmare. A congressional committee was shocked to find soldiers in rags, some even naked, and to see "feet and legs froze till they became black and it was often necessary to amputate them." The list of dying mounted.

Washington appealed to Congress. "No history now extant can furnish an instance of an army's suffering such uncommon hardships as ours has done and bearing them with the same patience and fortitude. To see men without blankets to lie on, without shoes (for the want of which their marches might be traced by the blood from their feet) and submitting without a murmur, is a proof of patience and obedience which in my opinion can scarce be paralleled." By mid-February, Washington warned that his army was failing fast. "I am now convinced beyond a doubt that unless some great and capital change suddenly takes place... this army must inevitably be reduced to one or other of these three things: starve, dissolve or disperse, in order to obtain subsistence."

Yet his leadership triumphed. The Continental army continued to harass British forces. For a few brief, heady days of summer in 1778, the English redcoats were driven back into New York City. France sent military advisors to assist Washington, and hopes revived. Some English businessmen, growing weary of the war and suggesting that "they are costing us more than they are earning for us," urged Parliament to let the colonies go.

Three years later, in October 1781, Washington's army, once again fighting over the same territory, threatened a British army just outside New York City. But when Washington learned that supporting French warships could blockade the nearby British garrison of Yorktown, Virginia, he sent his army racing south instead.

176

The British in Yorktown were caught napping. Seven thousand English soldiers surrendered, including the British commander of the Royal Expeditionary Forces himself, the portly Charles Cornwallis. As the band appropriately played, "The World Turned Upside Down," Cornwallis' sullen troops marched out and gave up their arms. It was the proverbial straw that broke the camel's back After five years of fighting, the effort had lost the support of the British public. The War for Independence was effectively over.

If the "impossible war" was now won, the task of forming a single nation from such diverse colonial societies was feared to be just as daunting. The general public needed a common denominator stronger than the provincial forces that tore them apart. History leaves no doubt that George Washington, the man, became that crucial common denominator. He was respected as a survivor, idolized as a war hero, and most important of all, he was trusted.

Noted historian, Page Smith, wrote of his bearing, his dignity, and the fact that he looked the part. "His genius was the ability to endure, to maintain his equilibrium in the midst of endless frustrations, disappointments , setbacks and defeats...." He was bound to create and sustain an army and in the process destroy, or at least mute, the deep rooted parochialism of the states. Thus, he not only symbolized the will of the Americans to persevere in the cause of liberty, he symbolized the unity of the states. If Washington's army had disintegrated, as it seemed so often on the verge of doing, Congress might well have followed suit. If Congress had disbanded, the problem of creating a viable nation out of thirteen disparate and jealous provinces would have been infinitely more difficult (consider the experience of Central and South America). Above all, if Washington had not, in his splendid erectness and his presence, embodied the union, it is doubtful that unification could have been accomplished on a practical political level.

What He Didn't Do

When a few years later a Constitutional Convention was called in Philadelphia, George Washington was promptly elected chairman. Among many, there was not much doubt that he would be called to lead whatever government the delegates finally selected. But when the Convention grew acrimonious and stalled, some members grew impatient, urging Washington to bring back his famous army and declare himself King. Historian, Allison Ford, suggests that such an option was very real and would have been highly popular. Washington's soldiers were still owed money from the Congress and would have fought for him to the death. There would have been immediate foreign support for such a decision. Monarchies in Europe were understandably threatened by all of the democratic rhetoric issuing out of the convention in Philadelphia. Most Christian clergy felt that the scriptures clearly sanctioned monarchies as "instruments of God." The apostle James had written, "obey the King." But there is no record that Washington ever considered such a possibility. Publicly and repeatedly he sternly rebuffed such suggestions. Wrote Page Smith, "in a sense it was Washington's restraint, more than his actions, that determined his greatness." Says Ford, "In the end, democracy was 'allowed to happen' by the generosity and integrity of one man." James Thomas Flexner, whose powerful portrait of Washington was a national best-seller, called him "The Indispensable Man."

Finally, after an election landslide on April 30, 1789, George Washington was sworn in as the first president of the newly formed United States of America. The ceremony was held in New York City. It was almost three hundred years after Christopher Columbus had landed in the "new world."

Looking tired and pale, Washington said little about the long American journey to independence, nor did he talk boldly about the future. Characteristically humble, the new president spoke mostly about God, solemnly telling the nation that, "It would be peculiarly improper to omit, in this first official act, my fervent supplication to that Almighty Being, who rules over the universe, who presides in the councils of nations, and whose providential aide can supply every human defect, that His benediction may consecrate to the liberties and happiness of the people of the United States... every step by which they have advanced to the character of an independent nation seems to have been distinguished by some token of providential agency... We ought to be no less persuaded that the propitious smiles of Heaven can never be expected on a nation that disregards the eternal rules of order and right, which Heaven itself has ordained."

After reelection in 1792, George Washington stepped down as the nation's first president. Some call it his most unselfish contribution to the country. The carefully crafted Constitution coming out of Philadelphia had allowed for a president to be reelected as often as he wished. Washington said that such power would ultimately be abused. Two terms in office were enough for any man.

Perhaps no other act endeared Washington to the nation and established his legend in history than his simple decision to walk away from power. The world had seen many conquerors like Alexander the Great, Julius Caesar and Ghengis Kahn. They would see many others such as Napoleon Bonaparte. All of them would cling to power till it was wrested from them, or in most cases, until they were killed. It is not natural to give up power. By his simple act, Washington assured that democracy would work and that the little Republic would survive him. He would be mentioned in history with heroic figures including Mahatma Ghandi, who placed ideal above personal power and prestige.

Two years after his retirement, George Washington lay dying at his home in Mount Vernon. He summoned his secretary to give last minute instructions, sighed, and then uttered his last words, "Tis well."

"Washington was the greatest man on earth," wrote Robert Morris, the Philadelphia patriot. North Carolina representative, William Hooper described him as "Superior to all... yet, utterly humble." But Major General Henry "Lighthorse Harry" Lee gave the most famous eulogy of all, saying that Washington was, "First in war, first in peace, and first in the hearts of his countrymen."

The concept of integrity, as embodied by America's first president quickly became a proud part of the national self-image. Robert E. Lee, Henry Lee's son and related through marriage to Washington, was taught it on his mother's knee. Andrew Carnegie invoked it as a part of his business philosophy, teaching managers that if you pay an employee more he will work up to the level of his new pay scale. When Franklin Moore tested the idea, he became even more wealthy than his employer, Carnegie. Napoleon Hill popularized it in his best-sellers.

George Washington was great and passionate, gigantic and troubling, controlled and unleashed. On those elements—both chained and explosive—rests the uniqueness of the experiment of these United States of America. Because of him, generations of patriots have continued to see that nothing is too difficult for the honorable.

CHARACTER

> *"The foundation of leadership is character."*
> *– General Alexander M. Patch*

Vision, courage, perseverance, and responsibility allow one to do great things, but history only holds one in high esteem if he or she manifests character. This is the foundation.

How you act around your friends, what you say to your subordinates, how you interact with your spouse in public, is not the real test of your character. It is who you are when no one sees you. Good character is reflected in who you are in private, the decisions you make that no one knows about, the things you do that will go unnoticed. It is impossible to be considered a person of good character if your actions contradict your words.

Many of the men and women we look to as leaders live their private lives differently than their public ones and expect us to overlook their transgressions. If you do not have character in one part of your life, then you simply do not possess character at all.

> *"It is sometimes frightening to observe the success which comes even to the outlaw with a polished technique...But I believe we must reckon with character in the end, for it is as potent a force in world conflict as it is in our own domestic affairs. It strikes the last blow in any battle."*
> *– Philip D. Reed*

For a time, there was a fashionable drift away from this philosophy, egged on by our increasing secularism and an almost obsessive public denial of any absolutes. Modern motivational writers, such as Robert Ringer, discounted the importance of character altogether. Life has shown that leadership without a foundation of integrity does not last. Business is coming back to this principle with a vengeance. You cannot fool people forever, not even yourself. A success that is here to stay, a leader who is to be revered, is built upon truth, not deception. George Washington came to personify this ideal of the American personality. However, it is a story that could have been written about any number of American heroes.

Where does character come from? If it is so important to my marriage, my health, and my business, how can I get some? Andrew Carnegie, the American steel magnate, and father of modern "success" books and tapes, believed that character could not be taught. He believed that it could only be exercised and developed like a muscle in the body. One does not wake up and vow to be a tower of moral strength and goodness like a George Washington. However, one does look for opportunities to practice honesty, fidelity, conscientiousness, and loyalty everyday. This is our "exercise."

"Character cannot be developed in ease and quiet. Only through experience of trial and suffering can the soul be strengthened, vision cleared, ambition inspired, and success achieved."
– Helen Keller

Chapter Seven

Our American Legacy

"Men make history and not the other way around. In periods where there is no leadership, society stands still. Progress occurs when courageous, skillful leaders seize the opportunity to change things for the better."
– Harry S Truman

Far from being a unique phenomenon in some mythic past, the pattern of sacrifice, courage, and victory illustrated in the lives of the Founding Fathers repeats itself time and again throughout the history of America.

The second generation of Americans had Daniel Boone, Davey Crockett, and William Henry Harrison. Had we chosen the Civil War for emphasis, we could have exemplified these same leadership qualities in the lives of Lincoln, Grant, and Lee. We could have climbed into an airplane with Wilbur and Orville Wright, Charles Lindbergh, or Amelia Earhart to experience a tree top view of the world with visionary men and women who were determined to achieve their dreams. At the turn of the century there was Teddy Roosevelt, Andrew Carnegie, the Rockefellers, and the Mellons.

We might have stumbled onto a bus in Montgomery, Alabama and sat next to Rosa Parks, a grandmother who had decided that, as an American, she had the right to sit where she chose, thus changing the color of the political process in America. Rosa Parks gave breath to Andrew Jackson's words, "One man with courage is a majority."

Recent decades have given us Bill Gates, Norman Schwartzkopf, Colin Powell, John Kennedy, and Ronald Reagan. We could also study the lives of millions of unsung heroes in America who are leading their families through crises, instilling in them the lessons of responsibility and character. The ability to lead is woven into the American personality.

> *"I see America, not in the setting sun of a black night of despair ahead of us, I see America in the crimson light of a rising sun fresh from the burning, creative hand of God. I see great days ahead, great days possible to men and women of will and vision..."* – *Carl Sandburg*

This is our America, built on a foundation of struggle, by men and women who have been, and still are, willing to lead their families to a greater tomorrow when everything appears hopeless. To take that for granted would be to deny us one of the defining qualities of the American spirit. Yet, it is this "taking for granted" that challenges us daily.

While we as a nation stand at the pinnacle as the most powerful, wealthy country on earth, many of our citizens believe they are faced with trials as never before. Violence, poverty, racism, and drug addiction sap at the very soul of this great republic.

Always Challenged

Yet, America has always been a violent place. Wild animals, severe weather, and native warriors defending their homeland, all have made for a hostile environment. The American Civil War cost us more casualties than World War I and World War II combined. The American West was often lawless and desperate. Nothing in our American experience, however, can quite explain the recent onslaught of American violence.

Every year in America, 23 million households are touched by crime. More than one million children each year are the victims of child abuse, most of them between the ages of two and five years old. Much of the rock and rap music our children listen to openly denigrates the police, the church, and women. Rape has increased 50% in the last decade.

While we are undoubtedly the richest nation on earth, our crime rate is almost 30 times greater than the People's Republic of China, and six times that of Japan. The solution offered by many Americans is simply to apprehend the criminals and lock them up. Today, following a prison-building spree in the 1990s, America houses more than 1.6 million inmates. Comparatively Great Britain has 55,000, Japan 54,000, and Denmark a mere 3,469.

Twelve million of our citizens live in poverty, teenage pregnancy is epidemic, bankruptcies are at an all-time high, and prescription drug addiction has increased 300% in the past twelve years.

Solutions to these problems are not simple ones. However, as mentioned in the introduction to this book, so much of who we are today is a result of the values instilled in us as children. What is it that we are teaching our children by our own examples? No one can dispute the fact that people are raised in different environments. Some environments are less nurturing, less conducive to emotional health. Some are simply abusive.

Fortunately, there is more to life than calculating the odds against overcoming poor starts. There is choice. No single person can easily change the odds that may be stacked against him, his family, his race, or his religion. Yet, every single human being is free to make his or her own decisions about the reactions to those circumstances. Clearly, there is no handicap, no pain, no prejudice that anyone in America is now suffering that isn't being overcome by someone else. Knowing it is possible strips us of the right to forfeit hope and thereby fail to succeed.

"Finish each day and be done with it...you have done what you could; some blunders and absurdities no doubt crept in; forget them as soon as you can. Tomorrow is a new day; you shall begin it well and serenely." – Ralph Waldo Emerson

---

Honorable leadership is not a Republican, Democrat, or Independent issue. It is not about the color of one's skin, nor the origins of one's ancestry. It does not matter which religious affiliation you claim. It is an issue for all Americans. It is not simply about our public pronouncements, but more importantly, it is about our private actions.

As each of us look back on our own lives, even if we come from a privileged background, there are many snapshots that we may wish were not a part of our life's photo album. There are certainly things, if given the chance, that we would do differently. However, that is one of the great things about America: we are a nation that allows one to try again. It is this that helps us to claim new heroes everyday.

Even though we are a land of heroes, it is not because we are without faults. Jefferson's record on slavery is debatable. There are rumors that he conducted a liaison with one of his teenage slave girls. Washington, while considered a great leader, is not viewed in the context of history as a military genius. Benjamin Franklin certainly led a life of questionable character as he sired children out of wedlock and pursued a mistress into his seventies. John Paul Jones was accused of murder.

A Land of Hope

If America is a land of heroic leaders it is because she is a land of regeneration. We believe that a man or woman can start over again. He or she can live down his or her mistakes and go on to do something constructive in life. Perhaps it was the endless living space and natural resources that inspired this notion. If a person failed in one village, he or she could always move on to the next. It was endless. A thief in one town could change and become the mayor of another town. America has always been a place of hope.

Our leaders survive in spite of mistakes and lapses in judgment because we forgive their errors and embrace their accomplishments. It is not just what they have done, but how we have chosen to interpret it that makes them larger than life, monuments to what we believe. In other words, it takes two to create a hero: the man or woman of action and the person who celebrates them.

We must never forget the responsibility placed at the feet of those individuals who are called upon to lead. However, it is equally important that their "followers" assume responsibility for their selection of "leaders." That selection will require them to utilize those same principles we are discussing in this book. Far too often, people shirk their role in decision making by attempting to affix blame for poor results on their "leaders." We are not exempt from the consequences of bad leadership because it is our decision whom we choose to follow.

It is the responsibility of each of us to instill in our young people the relevance of this nation's history. They need to know about the lives of George Washington, John Adams, Patrick Henry, and Thomas Jefferson. We need to teach them that the battle for our freedoms did not end with these leaders. They must understand that apathy can destroy hundreds of years of sacrifice.

In America, as history has proven, one person can make a difference. We must instill in our children an appreciation for our successes and failures. Their vocabulary should include both Yorktown and Bunker Hill; Ft. Sumter and Gettysburg; Pearl Harbor and Iwo Jim; Ia Dang Valley and the Tet Offensive. The words, "We hold these truths to be self-evident..." are words that should be second nature to them. Honorable leadership must be taught at all levels. In fact, in teaching these truths to our children we will reinforce them in ourselves.

On America's Future Leaders

"...we adults — parents and grandparents, teachers, coaches, clergy, scout leaders and others — must do our part. We cannot expect our kids to learn what is good and true from bad examples. Additionally, we must make certain that our children get the best education possible. Our children will not be able to cope or compete if they cannot read, communicate, or compute. We must do everything we can to keep them healthy — and that includes helping them understand the dangers of tobacco, drugs, and alcohol abuse. And, we must teach our children to honor those time-honored values that are not only a part of our culture, but also essential to individual success."
...Senator Orrin G. Hatch, Utah

"I do have faith in our young people to become the leaders of tomorrow...So long as we as a society are able to feed their eagerness and determination, I am confident that we will see leaders in government, industry, and all walks of life who are as accomplished and talented as those we recognize today. That is why I am confident about America's future."

...Senator Joseph R. Biden, Delaware

"I am concerned about the direction of our youth. Unfortunately, the people of this great nation tend to look cynically on all politicians and government in general. While a healthy dose of skepticism may be good for democracy, it seems unlikely that our form of government can survive in the absence of an informed and engaged citizenry. This is the challenge our nation faces in the next millennium...I remain fundamentally optimistic. American democracy is still the envy of the world, and our youth will surely meet the call of public service as have previous generations of Americans. It is rather up to those of us in positions of responsibility today to ensure that we bequeath to them the same legacy of freedom and opportunity with which we were blessed by our forefathers."

...Senator Paul D. Coverdell, Georgia

Final Thoughts

"My God! How little do my countrymen know what precious blessings they are in possession of, and which no other people on earth enjoy!" – Thomas Jefferson

We have an awesome responsibility to protect the freedoms that have been gained for us by the blood and tears of our ancestors. Personal liberty was won at a tremendous cost. Patriots of this newly formed Republic signed their own death warrants as they adopted the Declaration of Independence on July 4, 1776, and officially affixed their names to it during the next two months. This treasonous act to the King sent these liberators down a path that would allow no retreat. They knew what course they had chosen. We can only speculate, however, that they could not know the impact that such an action would have in the context of history.

The struggle for religious and personal freedoms that so aptly defined the battle for American independence was claimed by men and women of conviction. The patriots, oddly enough, comprised less than half of the population. As is typical of the American spirit, they believed that pursuing what was "right" was more important than what was "popular." They so precisely defined the leadership attributes of vision, courage, perseverance, responsibility, and character.

Those defining elements of leadership not only enabled these patriots to pursue their own freedom, but gave us the fundamentals of leadership on which to build our future, and the future of our children. It is so very important to understand that this country's freedoms are protected in so far as we are willing to maintain that same level of leadership in our own lives. Most of us will not be called on to forfeit our lives like they were willing to do in 1776, but we must govern our lives by the same principles.

"Posterity...you will never know how much it has cost my generation to preserve your freedom. I hope you will make good use of it." – John Quincy Adams

---

Acknowledgments

Writing this book has proven to be quite an undertaking. As I began to weave my way through the process I quickly learned that this is a team effort. Therefore, let me take this opportunity to extend a sincere thank you to those people who have made this a reality.

I am honored for the input of several esteemed members of the United States Senate who were very helpful in offering a contemporary perspective on leadership. To Senators Strom Thurmond, Richard Shelby, Jesse Helms, Orrin Hatch, Paul Coverdell, and Joseph Biden, I say thank you for your time and thoughtfulness. A special thank you to Senator Strom Thurmond for writing the foreword. I have known the Senator for most of my life and have a deeper respect for this nation because of him.

One individual who deserves a great deal of personal praise is my good friend Matthew Sweetanos. Your dedication to this project was critical to its success. I would also like to thank Doug Wead for his help in steering many of my thoughts and ideas onto the printed page. You have been a good friend. Thank you for your time and talent. Additionally, I would like to offer my gratitude to Jill Roberts, Larry Sweat, Shad and Elise Helmstetter, and my dearest friend Tom Wille.

Thank you to the men and women at the Russ Reid Company for their guidance. They include Mark McIntyre, Jovita Vergara, Peter Arnold, and Rachel Krajc.

As all of the royalties from the sale of this book are being donated to the American Leadership Foundation, it is critical to thank those great Americans who sit on its Board of Advisors. Words can never express my gratitude for your

197

willingness to participate in helping deliver our message. They include:

Senator Spencer Abraham
United States Senator, Michigan
John E. Bianchi
former Chairman of the Board, Bianchi International
Arnold I. Burns
former Deputy Attorney General,
United States Department of Justice
Robbie Callaway
Senior Vice President, Boys and Girls Clubs of America
Governor Carroll Campbell
former Governor, South Carolina
Billy Childers
Chief Executive Officer, Childers Enterprises, Inc.
Senator Max Cleland
United States Senator, Georgia
Senator Daniel K. Inouye
United States Senator, Hawaii
Sonny Jurgensen
Hall of Fame Quarterback, Washington Redskins
Ronald C. Kaufman
former Assistant to President Bush,
White House Senior Staff
John C. Lawn
Chairman, The Century Council;
former Director, Drug Enforcement Administration
Senator Trent Lott
Majority Leader, United States Senate
Admiral Thomas H. Moorer
former Chairman, Joint Chiefs of Staff
Elaine B. Rogers
President, USO – Washington, D.C.
Senator Strom Thurmond
President Pro Tempore, United States Senate
Lt. General Claudius E. Watts III (Ret)
former President, The Citadel
Armstrong Williams
Nationally Syndicated Columnist

I would like to express my appreciation and respect to my in-laws, Leonard and LaVerne Bartolutti. You have entrusted your daughter into my care. I hope I never disappoint you. I have always admired your character and value your friendship.

Most importantly, I want to thank my parents, Duke and Elaine Short, for instilling in me the values presented in this book. Your belief in God and your faith in America has taught me to stand strong in my convictions.

And finally, to those Americans whose sacrifices gave us the opportunity to lead as free men and women. You are America.

References

Allan, Herbert S. *John Hancock (Patriot in Purple)*; The Beechhurst Press, New York. 1953.

Baron, Robert C. *Jefferson The Man (In His Own Words)*; Fulcrum/ Starwood Publishing in association with the Library of Congress, Colorado and Washington D.C. 1993.

Brodie, Fawn M. *Thomas Jefferson (An Intimate History)*; W.W. Norton and Company, New York. 1974.

Collier, Christopher and James Lincoln. *Decision in Philadelphia*; Random House and Reader's Digest Press, New York. 1986.

Fitton, Robert A. *Leadership (Quotations from the World's Greatest Motivators)*; Westview Press, Colorado. 1997.

Flexner, James Thomas. *Washington (The Indispensable Man)*; Little, Brown and Company, Boston and Toronto. 1974.

Fowler, Jr., William M. *The Baron of Beacon Hill (a Biography of John Hancock)*; Houghton Mifflin Company, Boston. 1980.

Garrison, Webb. *Great Stories of the American Revolution*; Rutledge Hill Press, Tennessee. 1990.

Gipson, Lawrence Henry. *The Coming of the Revolution*; Harper & Row, New York and Evanston. 1954.

Hart, Benjamin. *Faith & Freedom*; Lewis and Stanley, Dallas. 1988.

Hunt, John Gabriel. *Words of Our Nation*; Portland House, New Jersey. 1993.

Kennedy, Roger G. *Orders From France*; Alfred A. Knopf, New York. 1989.

McLaughlin, Jack. *Jefferson and Monticello*; Henry Holt and Company, New York. 1988.

Morison, Samuel Eliot. *John Paul Jones (a Sailor's Biography)*; Little, Brown and Company, Boston and Toronto. 1959.

Randall, Willard Sterne. *Thomas Jefferson (a Life)*; Henry Holt and Company, New York. 1993

Russell, Phillips. *Benjamin Franklin (the First Civilized American)*; Blue Ribbon Books, New York. 1926.

Russell, Robert Wallace. *Washington Shall Hang*; Theo. Gaus' Sons, New York. 1976.

Skousen, W. Cleon. *The Making of America (the Substance and Meaning of the Constitution)*; National Center for Constitutional Studies, Washington, D.C. 1985.

The Editors of Newsweek Books. *Thomas Jefferson (A Biography in His Own Words)*; Newsweek, New York. 1974.

Various Authors. *The Spirit of Seventy-Six (The Story of the American Revolution as Told by Participants)*; Harper and Row Publishers, New York, Evanston, San Francisco, and London. 1975.

EXCALIBUR PRESS is proud to announce the upcoming release of *WE STILL BELIEVE – America's Legacy of Hope* by Bo Short, President of the American Leadership Foundation.

Once again, Bo Short inspires us to live up to our potential. He looks at the challenges we face in today's America, and offers practical, illuminating ways to achieve. Bo Short shines the spotlight on the power of hope that makes America great.

Look for *WE STILL BELIEVE – America's Legacy of Hope* in bookstores in the fall of 1998.

EXCALIBUR
PRESS

American Leadership Foundation

The American Leadership Foundation is a not-for-profit organization dedicated to instilling and renewing the values of leadership in all Americans. The Foundation's mission is to nurture honorable leadership by promoting vision, courage, perseverance, responsibility and character.

Whether leading a nation, a business or a family, the ability to achieve our most cherished dreams rests with our willingness to embrace the virtues and values of leadership. Therefore, the Foundation is putting leadership at the forefront of the American agenda through a variety of inspirational and instructional programs. Some of them include: a speakers bureau, mentor program, college scholarships, regional leadership conferences and a national awards program.

PRAISE FOR THE
American Leadership Foundation

"I have always believed that for one to succeed, he or she must possess certain leadership qualities. That is why it is imperative that we provide our young men and women with the necessary leadership qualities. Your organization assists in providing these qualities to our youth, and I would be proud to be a member of the Advisory Board."

...**Senator Trent Lott**
Majority Leader, United States Senate

"In the Chinese language, the written characters for 'challenge' and 'opportunity' are the same. I believe that summarizes America's situation today. It also shows why the work of the American Leadership Foundation is so important. The Foundation is giving the next generation of Americans the inspiration and tools necessary to triumph over adversity."

...Elaine B. Rogers
President, USO – Washington, D.C.

"Perseverance. Character. Values. If there are any better qualities to instill in tomorrow's leaders, I am not familiar with them. The American Leadership Foundation is promoting all of these on behalf of talented American men and women. That's why I'm proud to be involved."

...Senator Daniel K. Inouye
United States Senator, Hawaii

"With the pace of change in American society becoming increasingly rapid, tomorrow's leaders will need special training and expertise. The American Leadership Foundation is committed to spurring this process on — and in the process, create benefits for every American citizen."

...Robbie Callaway
Senior Vice President, Boys and Girls Clubs of America

"America is faced with unprecedented global opportunities. Yet we will only be able to seize these opportunities if we have leaders of all ages ready to excel and succeed. That's why I've joined the American Leadership Foundation — because it is committed to instilling and nurturing the values of leadership in today's society."

...**Senator Spencer Abraham**
United States Senator, Michigan

For more information on the
American Leadership Foundation
please call or write:

1300 I Street N.W.
Suite 250 West
Washington, D.C. 20005
Phone: (202) 216-9104
Fax: (202) 842-3492
www.americanleadership.org